"This complex issue affects the lives of millions of people and their families every day. Christopher and Beverly should be applauded for approaching a delicate subject with true compassion."

—**MARIA SHRIVER**

"One of the best books available on codependency. . . . Here you will learn how to return to compassion and how to back off without backing out of a relationship altogether."

—**DR. DREW PINKSY**

"*When Your Partner Has an Addiction* is a godsend for the millions who feel trapped between hope and despair. . . . Lawford writes with elegance, wisdom, and compassion in a guide that can change—even save—your life."

—**DAVID SHEFF**, *New York Times* bestselling author of *Beautiful Boy* and *Clean*

"*When Your Partner Has an Addiction* is a terrific primer for dealing with a practicing addict that respects both partners' struggle with codependency. It provides practical solutions to avoid enabling and shows how to be a compassionate supporter of your loved one."

—**DARLENE LANCER**, author of *Codependency for Dummies* and *Conquering Shame and Codependency: 8 Steps to Freeing the True You*

"In this eminently readable and valuable book, Christopher Lawford reminds all of us—husbands and wives, parents and grandparents, counselors and physicians—that addiction and recovery are family affairs and it takes a family to help the addict recover and live a sober, happy, and satisfying life."

—**JOSEPH A. CALIFANO, JR.**, founder of the National Center on Addiction and Substance Abuse at Columbia University and former US Secretary of Health, Education, and Welfare

WHEN
YOUR PARTNER
HAS AN
ADDICTION

WHEN YOUR PARTNER HAS AN ADDICTION

How Compassion Can
Transform Your Relationship
(and Heal You Both in the Process)

CHRISTOPHER KENNEDY LAWFORD
AND BEVERLY ENGEL

BenBella Books, Inc.
Dallas, TX

BenBella Books, Inc.
10440 N. Central Expressway, Suite 800 | Dallas, TX 75231
www.benbellabooks.com | Send feedback to feedback@benbellabooks.com

Printed in the United States of America
10 9 8 7 6 5 4 4 3 2 1

Library of Congress Cataloging-in-Publication Data
Names: Lawford, Christopher Kennedy, 1955- author. | Engel, Beverly, author.
Title: When your partner has an addiction : how compassion can transform your
  relationship (and heal you both in the process) / Christopher Kennedy
  Lawford, with Beverly Engel.
Description: Dallas, TX : BenBella Books, [2016] | Includes bibliographical
  references and index.
Identifiers: LCCN 2016016223 (print) | LCCN 2016025774 (ebook) | ISBN
  9781941631867 (paperback) | ISBN 9781941631874 (electronic)
Subjects: LCSH: Addicts—Rehabilitation. | Addicts—Family relationships. |
  Codependency. | BISAC: SELF-HELP / Codependency. | SELF-HELP / Adult
  Children of Substance Abusers. | FAMILY & RELATIONSHIPS / Marriage.
Classification: LCC HV4998 .L3943 2016 (print) | LCC HV4998 (ebook) | DDC
  362.29/13—dc23
LC record available at https://lccn.loc.gov/2016016223

Editing by Leah Wilson
Copyediting by Karen Wise
Proofreading by James Fraleigh and Kimberly Broderick
Text design and composition by Silver Feather Design
Front cover by Kit Sweeney
Full cover by Sarah Dombrowsky
Printed by Lake Book Manufacturing

Distributed by Perseus Distribution | www.perseusdistribution.com
To place orders through Perseus Distribution:
Tel: (800) 343-4499 | Fax: (800) 351-5073 | E-mail: orderentry@perseusbooks.com

Special discounts for bulk sales (minimum of 25 copies) are available.
Please contact Aida Herrera at aida@benbellabooks.com.

Contents

Introduction

FROM CHRIS

That amazing human interaction we call romantic love can be magical. But relationships are also challenging; even in the best of circumstances, they can be as rife with pitfalls as they are with possibilities. When you add addiction to the mix, you have the potential for frustration, anger, and pain—in a word, failure.

But it doesn't have to be that way, and that's what these pages will show.

The most important qualification I have for coauthoring a book about relationships with individuals recovering from substance or behavioral addiction is my own experience recovering from these disorders for the past thirty years. As a person in long-term recovery, I've found that maintaining solid, fulfilling relationships has been an enormous challenge, though I've never stopped trying. Maybe that's why relationships and human development are so fascinating to me. And that fascination is one of the reasons I do the work I do today.

After spending twenty years in the film and television industries as an actor, lawyer, executive, and producer, I wrote three *New York Times* bestselling books dealing with addiction, *Symptoms of Withdrawal* (2005), *Moments of Clarity* (2009), and *Recover to Live* (2013), and, more recently, *What Addicts Know* (2014). I have campaigned tirelessly on behalf of the recovery community in both the public and private sectors, holding appointed positions with the California

Public Health Advisory Committee and serving as goodwill ambassador for the United Nations Office on Drugs and Crime to promote activities supporting drug treatment, care, and recovery. In addition, I earned a master's certification in clinical psychology from Harvard Medical School, where I held an academic appointment as a lecturer in psychiatry, and I currently speak around the world on issues related to addiction and mental health.

Recovery from any addiction, as I know too well from my own experience and from the stories I've heard from others in my work, is a lifelong process. The learning never ends. It takes most of us a lifetime to establish and maintain a stable, mutually nurturing, and rewarding relationship with someone we love and, even then, we don't always do it well. The past traumas and family of origin dysfunction that cause or contribute to addiction, the fanciful thinking, and sometimes just the stuff we arrive on the planet with often combine to derail our most ardent and committed intentions. This is why having compassion for your partner is so important. No one consciously chooses addiction to a substance or a behavior over his partner. There are always reasons—powerful ones—why a person retreats into addiction. Understanding that not only adds to your compassion, but brings you closer to experiencing true intimacy with your partner.

There was a time when I believed that a person in recovery who had successfully put away the chemicals was destined to find the love of his life and live happily ever after. I was wrong. It took my first fourteen years of recovery before I fully grasped how profound my issues were in the realm of love, sex, and intimacy. Addiction is often a solution, if a poor one, to deeper issues; those of us who struggle with substance or behavioral addiction are either medicating the intolerableness of our existence or trying to touch the hand of God in an insatiable quest for a more thrilling life. Love and relationships can be used in the same way. But they don't have to be.

You can't make someone get help or go into recovery when they don't want to do it. Pushing, prodding, threatening—they don't work. Putting that kind of pressure on someone usually just makes things worse. Why? Because they aren't ready. I believe that all of us, not just people struggling with addiction, get intermittent windows of opportunity to change our lives. We wake up one day and something happens that allows us to say to ourselves: I'm going to change my life. *I'm going to get sober. I'm going to be a good father and a good husband.* I tried everything on the planet to get sober for about nine years. I was significantly motivated to change my life, yet I still couldn't do it. Then one day I saw a window of opportunity and I crawled through. I can tell you from experience that when that window opens, you need all the motivation and all the tools you can muster in that moment to crawl through. Whatever gets you there is good. And love can be a powerful motivator.

This book will show you how your actions—your love and compassion—can help your partner take advantage of his* windows for change, and fortify him for the challenges he'll face in recovery. We won't excuse or minimize the harm and pain he has caused you. But we do want to bring hope and promise back into your lives, and strength and possibility into your relationship.

You're in a relationship with someone who struggles with addiction, so you already know it's hard. What you might not yet know is why. Most of us don't ever closely examine why we choose the people

---

* Throughout this book, we've used the pronoun "he" for those who suffer from a substance or activity dependency. This is done for simplicity's sake only. We recognize that there are also many women who suffer from dependency and addiction problems and that their partners are in just as much need of this book. In addition, although all the case examples in the book are male-female couples and we often use "she" in referring to the partners of those who suffer from substance or activity dependency, the information in this book applies to any couple, regardless of its members' genders.

we do to populate our lives. We're intimidated, and hesitant to ask the penetrating questions. We prefer not to look too closely at where we came from and at what effect the baggage we inherited has on those we choose to love. Making the choice to stay with your partner means confronting those things head-on.

Believe me, it's a hard road. There's an easier one: Kick your partner to the curb and try to move on. There are situations where you absolutely should do this; we'll discuss those in this book. But in many cases, taking that easy road is not going to get you a profound human experience. It's not necessarily going to help *you*.

If you picked a person with an addiction to be in relationship with, you probably have some issues of your own. You picked your current partner for a reason, and until you understand that reason and take responsibility for the ways in which you've co-created your situation, you're just going to pick people like him over and over again. You have the choice to leave, but you will end up back here again.

The good news is that your partner is giving you an opportunity to deal with your issues. People who struggle with addiction have a way of lifting up a mirror to everyone they have relationships with, thereby revealing others' dysfunctions. Your partner will show you yours, and if he is in recovery, doing the work to change, he will challenge you to change as well. (Marriages that break up once a partner gets sober often do so because the other person isn't ready to look at their own issues.) By staying and helping your partner, especially if you follow the guidance in this book, you'll be helping yourself as well. You will begin the process of revealing your own authentic humanness. And the rewards for that journey can be greater than you ever imagined or could have predicted. Being involved in your partner's recovery can be one of the greatest emotional, spiritual, and physical experiences of your life.

Relationships are confusing, they're exhausting, they're risky. But that's how we learn how to be better human beings. There is no greater classroom on humanity than the classroom of a relationship, and learning how to be in an intimate, loving partnership is the PhD program of becoming a fully realized human being. You may have picked up this book because you wanted to help your partner and improve your relationship—and we'll show you how to do that. But we'll also show you how to better understand yourself, and begin to live a more fulfilled and meaningful life.

This book shows you how to be in a relationship without being hopelessly codependent. It shows you how to be a true partner to someone whose secrecy and isolation often feel insurmountable. And it shows you, above all, how compassion can change your relationship, and your life.

FROM BEVERLY

If you are married to or romantically involved with someone who is dependent on alcohol or drugs or suffers from compulsive behavior, including gambling, shopping, sex, pornography, overeating, or work, and you want to discover the best ways to help him, this book is for you.

You may have read other books about being in a relationship with someone struggling with addiction. But this book will be unlike anything you've read before. We will not blame you for your partner's problems or tell you that you are "enabling" him if you continue to support him. Instead of telling you to either stand aside or run away, we are going to tell you how you can walk beside your partner and help him on his journey to recovery—without falling into the trap of being codependent.

In these pages we challenge the way society looks at those who are dependent on a substance or an activity; instead of demonizing them, we take a close look at why they are who they are and do what they do. We pull back the bandages of addiction and look at the wounds underneath in order to help you gain true compassion for your addicted partner's suffering. And instead of focusing on their flaws, we look at their strengths and their gifts.

We also challenge the way society looks at the partners of those who are dependent on a substance or activity. Instead of viewing them as long-suffering victims who put up with unacceptable behavior because they themselves are flawed or inadequate or desperate to not be alone, we focus on their strengths and gifts as well, and share strategies for redirecting those strengths and gifts to help heal their own wounds as well as their partners'.

You'll learn skills that will help you communicate more effectively, more positively, and more compassionately, so you can transform your relationship with your partner. You'll also discover, as Chris said, why you chose your partner in the first place and what you need to learn about yourself in order to change your own unhealthy thinking and behavior.

Like many other partners of someone with a dependence problem, you may feel a longing to bring up the issue of your partner's addiction but are afraid to broach the subject. You may fear angering him or making the situation worse. You may have tried before only to be rebuffed or blamed for his problems. In this book we will help you learn how to let your partner know you are concerned without shaming him or making him angry, and how to communicate with him in a way that will encourage him to listen. Then, once your partner is open to hearing you, you can try our strategies for helping him in his efforts to stop his unhealthy behaviors. In these pages we share the most up-to-date research about substance and activity dependence, what works and what doesn't as far as recovery is concerned, as well as the most effective avenues for recovery, so you can pass on this information to your partner.

The typical advice given to partners of those suffering from an addiction is to either end the relationship or stop trying to change the addict and accept him the way he is. This book offers you a third option: becoming your partner's supporter or collaborator as he makes changes for himself. We want to let you know that you can, in fact, help your loved one change. And we will show you, step by step, how to go about it.

While the information we offer doesn't contradict what you might learn at an Al-Anon or Co-Dependents Anonymous (CoDA) meeting, it will add to what you may think you know about those who are addicted and how to relate to them. It takes the Al-Anon message one step further, helping you love your partner in a deeper, more compassionate way.

For those of you who have nearly reached your limit in terms of how much you can take, we offer suggestions that will help you *back off* without *backing out* of the relationship altogether. We will help you communicate your limits without arguing, yelling, or resorting to emotional blackmail. And for those of you who are truly on the fence, we will help you make a decision you can live with and not regret. Most importantly, we will help you do all this while taking care of *yourself* in the process.

We offer exercises throughout the book, and it has been our experience that those who complete the exercises tend to benefit more than those who don't. Overall, however, we encourage you to take in what seems beneficial to you and bypass anything that doesn't.

I come to this project with thirty-five years of experience working with hundreds of couples as a psychotherapist and a marriage and family therapist. One of the primary reasons couples come to see me is because one partner has an addiction or dependence problem and the other doesn't know whether to stay in the relationship or end it. I am also one of the world's leading experts in the treatment of emotional abuse, something partners of those with dependence problems are often dealing with. In this book I offer you the same advice I offer my clients, as well as provide some case examples in order to help you recognize that you are not alone.

One thing I discovered in my work with such couples, well before the connection became recognized and accepted in the addiction field, was that those who were abused or neglected in childhood are far more likely to become addicted or dependent on alcohol or drugs than the rest of the population. So, while I am not an addiction expert—that's Chris—I *am* an expert in helping those who were abused or neglected make that all-important connection between the abuse they experienced in childhood and their addiction, and realize that it is *understandable* that they would turn to a substance or an activity as a way of coping with the trauma they experienced. Realizing this can be the difference between continuing to blame and shame themselves and gaining self-compassion—an essential step in recovering from the abuse and from the way they chose to self-medicate.

I've seen, over and over, in my clients as well as in the research, the difference that compassion can make in a person's life. And in this book, I use my experience to help you offer your partner compassion and understanding in a way that can save not only his life, but yours as well.

PART I.

LOVE, COMPASSION, AND UNDERSTANDING

CHAPTER 1

Love and Addiction: Can They Coexist?

"In real love you want the other person's good. In romantic love you want the other person."
—Margaret Anderson

IT CAN BE HARD TO LOVE SOMEONE WHO HAS AN ADDICTION. How do you love someone who lies to you, constantly disappoints you, and seems to value alcohol, drugs, work, or another addiction over you?

It's also difficult to love someone who seems like two different people—kind and loving when he isn't using, angry and defensive when he is. Someone who blames his addiction and everything else that goes wrong in his life on you—and refuses to face the truth about himself and his addiction.

But if you are reading this book, it probably means that you do still love your partner. That despite hurt after hurt, disappointment after disappointment, and betrayal after betrayal, and despite days where it just doesn't feel worthwhile to keep up the fight, you haven't quite reached the point where you want to give up. You are still looking for a way to help your partner. If this is your situation, this book is for you.

More than anything else, this book is about compassion. It is about gaining empathy for and understanding of a partner who is dependent on a substance (alcohol, drugs, food) or an activity (gambling, shopping, sex, work). It is about avoiding falling into the trap of codependency—or, if you already have fallen, learning how to replace that codependency with compassion. And it is about allowing yourself to have compassion for yourself in a way that leads to healing in your own life and opens the door for healthier relationships.

But this book is also, most importantly, about love—how your love for your partner, and his love for you, can contribute to his recovery.

Maybe you've heard that those who suffer from an addiction are selfish, egotistical, and narcissistic, and don't really have the capacity to love anyone else. Maybe you've heard that an addict's primary relationship is with his mind-altering chemical or his compulsive behavior at the expense of other relationships—that the only thing he *really* loves is his booze or his drugs or his sex or his gambling.

You've probably also heard that partners of those who are substance dependent are by definition codependent, meaning that they are also addicted—but to love. And you may have been told that your behavior is characterized more by neediness, control, manipulation, and resentment than by true love, and that the best thing you can do for your partner and yourself is to walk away.

While there are certainly some truths to the stereotypes about substance-dependent people and their partners, they are far from absolute. Many who suffer from an addiction truly love their partners and their children, want the best for them, and feel deep shame and regret for their actions and inactions when their addiction takes over. It is as if there is a giant wall between who they are and who they want to be, and they just can't figure out how to get over that wall. For these people, the capacity to love is there; their addiction just prevents them from expressing it. As one of Beverly's clients who was actively in recovery from an addiction to cocaine told her, "I did love people when I was actively using. But I loved to get high more."

Far from being unable to love, those who are substance or activity dependent can be extremely sensitive people who are capable of loving very deeply. In fact, they are often so sensitive that they use alcohol, drugs, food, sex, gambling, or work to protect themselves from opening up, becoming too vulnerable, and getting hurt. They are often so broken by past trauma that they are afraid to admit to themselves or others how deeply they *do* love.

Those considered codependent can also be extremely sensitive, loving human beings whose issues prevent them from having a healthy relationship with their partner. In fact, as we'll see, many substance-dependent and codependent individuals encounter similar obstacles when it comes to the ability to love—and can have similar reasons, often rooted in past trauma, for those obstacles.

In fact, many addicts and codependents are drawn to each other for this very reason: They recognize a kindred soul.

OBSTACLES TO BEING ABLE TO LOVE

The most powerful obstacle in the way of addicts' and codependents' ability to love is that both find it difficult to love themselves.

This lack of self-love—commonly referred to as low self-esteem—is often the result of not having been adequately loved by their parents or primary caretakers during childhood. If a mother does not emotionally bond with her child, or if she emotionally neglects her child (by offering little to no affection, nurturing, or encouragement), the child feels this lack of emotional connection and experiences it as a deep loss.

If that same child experiences love from even one other person—a father, a grandmother, a sibling, a family friend, a teacher—it can make a difference not only in the child's ability to love someone else, but also in his or her mental health. A child who is not loved, nurtured, and accepted by either or both parents can carry feelings of inadequacy, shame, and even self-hatred into adulthood. While such people may be able to love others, they often still find it difficult or even impossible to love themselves—and this will inevitably affect their relationships.

Filling Up the Emptiness

Some people suffered such extreme neglect or abandonment in childhood that they feel empty inside, and experience such an intense craving for love that no one person can fill them up. This craving for love is often what brings together those who are addicted to a substance or an activity and their codependent partners: Each is looking to the other to give them the love they didn't receive as children. This same craving manifests in both a codependent's need to never be alone and an addicted person's use of their addiction. The codependent is looking for the other person to fill that emptiness, while the addict is looking to a substance or activity to do the same.

Those who suffer from feelings of emptiness can also become addicted to the feeling of falling in love, often referred to as a "love addiction." Rather than develop real relationships of depth and meaning, these people are always searching for the euphoric feeling that comes with the honeymoon phase of every new relationship, a feeling characterized by *intensity* rather than *intimacy*. True intimacy takes time and happens through the development of a healthy relationship; constantly seeking intensity more often leads to emotional chaos and does not fulfill the person's need to be loved.

An Inability to Connect with Others

Not adequately bonding with a caregiver by the age of two or experiencing neglect as an infant or young child doesn't just become an obstacle to loving yourself. It also has an effect on the right frontal lobe of your brain—the area that determines how you connect with other people. This early "relational trauma" may last a lifetime, making it difficult to connect with anyone without enormous pain and dysfunction. Relational trauma can set a person up for codependency, addiction, and destructive relational patterns, as well as self-esteem issues.

The research of pioneering clinical scientist Dr. Allan Schore of the Department of Psychiatry and Biobehavioral Sciences at UCLA's Geffen School of Medicine has shown that in response to a caregiver's neglect, an infant develops one of two response patterns: hyperarousal (from experiencing high levels of anxiety) or dissociation (from feelings of disconnect from self or surroundings). Either of these relational trauma patterns can be associated with an inability to self-regulate the intensity and duration of emotional states, which results in a compulsion for self-medicating later in life.

Dr. van der Kolk also did research concerning how attachment failures can create difficulties in developing healthy relationships. He refers to this as Developmental Trauma Disorder (DTD) and lists its symptoms as relational and chronic: inability to concentrate and regulate emotions; anger, fear, and anxiety; self-loathing; aggression; and self-destructive behavior.

Fear of Intimacy

Even if a person is capable of loving a partner, it does not mean they will do so. Many substance-dependent people, as well as many codependents, are afraid of intimacy. While each may long for love, they may—ironically—be unable to return it. They are so afraid of being rejected or abandoned the way they were as a child that they can't risk opening their heart.

Focusing attention on a substance or activity is one effective way of avoiding intimacy, as is continually becoming involved with "unavailable" partners (partners who are married, those addicted to alcohol or drugs, workaholics). Constantly focusing on the reasons why one's partner can't be trusted is yet another.

The Walls That Shame Built

Shame is another major deterrent to being able to love—both oneself and someone else.

Those who were abused in childhood in particular often suffer from a great deal of shame. Shame is a natural reaction to abuse, as abuse—and the accompanying feelings of violation and helplessness—is by nature humiliating and dehumanizing.

This isn't true just for physical and sexual attacks. Constant criticism, name-calling, belittling, unreasonable expectations, and other forms of emotional abuse can be just as harmful and just as shame inducing. Neglect can also create shame in a child, causing him or her to think: *If even my own mother doesn't love me enough to take care of me, I must be worthless.*

Some have suffered so much shame that they cannot let in anything good—including love. They push away anyone who loves them, and they sabotage good relationships. Some people experience so much shame in childhood that they build up a defensive wall to prevent ever feeling shamed again. But as long as that wall is up, they can't really love.

THE TRANSFORMATIVE POWER OF LOVE

When addicts and codependents can overcome these obstacles and truly love another person, however, that love can transform their lives.

Sometimes, when a couple falls deeply in love, their love is so strong that it seems to make anything possible—even surviving a substance dependency. In fact, sometimes the love a substance-dependent person has for another person can be so strong that it transforms his life.

Here's what Beverly's client Larry has to say about being transformed by love:

> When I met Rhonda I was a full-blown alcoholic. I couldn't get through the day without getting drunk. I met Rhonda at a party where we were both drinking, so she didn't notice that I had a problem. We had one of those intense nights where we both fell in love and couldn't keep our hands off each other. I spent the night at her house that very first night and we were a couple from that day forward.
>
> But about two months into our relationship Rhonda sat me down and said that she wasn't going to be able to stay with me if I continued drinking at my present pace. She said that she loved to party with me once in a while but that I seemed to need to get drunk every day and she just couldn't tolerate that. She said that she'd be patient while I worked on myself and did whatever I needed to do to cut back on the drinking but that she wouldn't stay with me indefinitely.
>
> I was devastated at the idea of losing her. I'd never loved anyone so deeply and completely before. And no one had loved me as much. No one had been as kind and generous and loving with me. So, I sat myself down and gave myself a good talking-to. I told myself that it was up to me: I could either lose the best thing in my life or I could stop drinking. Believe it or not, I chose to stop drinking—cold turkey, right there and then. I haven't had a drop since.

While stories of such dramatic turnarounds aren't the norm, they also aren't unheard of.

Love can also motivate smaller, but still important, changes, such as keeping a dependency from taking over one's life in order to support one's family. Beverly's mother, a single parent, loved her enough to limit her alcohol use to evenings and her days off so she could go to work and support the family. In other words, she loved Beverly enough to become what is often called a "functioning alcoholic." She often shared with Beverly that before she became a mother she was an extremely selfish person and that having Beverly taught her how to love.

Sometimes love can be so powerful that it can even help heal the wounds of childhood. This can be a powerful experience.

> *Beverly: When I was in my mid-thirties I met a man who had a similar background to mine. He too suffered from neglect and criticism from his mother and, in addition, she also physically abandoned him when he was six years old, leaving him with a family friend. As is common for couples who are falling in love, we shared our stories with each other. Discovering that there was someone else in the world who had experienced the same pain and feelings of worthlessness felt like a gift to both of us.*
>
> *We were together for eight years, and during that time we both experienced a great deal of healing. We would watch movies on TV together and at the end, we would often cry in each other's arms. For the first time in our lives we had someone to comfort us.*
>
> *Although the relationship eventually ended, it did so because we had become too dependent on each other and each of us needed to be alone in order to "find ourselves." We remain extremely close friends, even after all these years, and the reason is we really love each other. We are both extremely grateful that we had someone in our lives who truly loved us and accepted us the way we were during that crucial time of healing. Our relationship has been the catalyst for powerful healing in both our lives.*

We believe that no one is beyond redemption. Love, understanding, and compassion can heal even the most damaged souls. The love you have for your partner can help him bring down his walls, open up, and take the risk of loving you back. And his love for you can do the same. But it is not the entire answer. You will learn as you continue reading this book that you each need to learn to overcome any obstacles to loving yourselves as well.

HOW DO I KNOW IF HE REALLY LOVES ME?

Maybe you're asking yourself: *How do I know if he loves me? He says he does, but he lies so much—how do I know if he's just lying to me to get me to stay?*

It's true that there are some addicts who perpetually lie, including telling a woman they love her when they are actually just manipulating her.

Some in the recovery movement believe that it is essential for your partner's behavior to match his words, and that otherwise you are allowing yourself to be manipulated, controlled, and deceived. No doubt you've heard the expression "talk is cheap." But if you are at a place where you no longer believe the words "I love you," what behaviors are proof of your partner's love?

Some of you may answer, "If he truly loved me he would go into treatment," and there are some addicts who do finally decide to begin a twelve-step or other program in order to show their partner they love them. But, generally speaking, deciding *not* to enter treatment is not an indication that your partner doesn't love you. He may love you but simply not be ready to take this step. (Later, we'll be discussing ways that you can encourage your partner to seek help without giving him an ultimatum or insisting that doing so is the only way to prove his love to you.)

So, how does a person act when he really loves you? There is no one answer to this question—especially when it comes to someone with a dependency. Your partner may treat you with respect, kindness, and consideration (all standard indications of love) most of the time—that is, unless he is using. Then he may turn into a completely different person, saying cruel things, disregarding your feelings, or disrespecting you in front of others. Does this mean that he doesn't really love you, or does it mean that he is projecting his own self-hatred onto you? Does it mean that he isn't being genuine when he treats you with respect, kindness, and consideration the rest of the time? There are no easy answers here.

When someone is overtaken by a strong compulsion to drink or take drugs, to gamble or to seek an illicit sexual release, his concern for others—even others he loves—gets lost. It's not necessarily the case that he doesn't love you and care about your needs or your happiness—it's just that he hasn't found a way to deal with his compulsion. It likely has nothing to do with his love for you.

Beverly once asked a very wise therapist, "How do you know if you can trust someone?" Her answer? "The real question isn't whether or not you can *trust the other person*. It's whether you can *trust yourself* to take care of yourself with this person."

> *Beverly: From that time on, this was the question I asked myself whenever I was uncertain about a relationship: "Can I trust myself with this person? Can I trust myself to take care of myself with this person?" Sometimes the answer was a clear no, and I realized that I had stopped standing up for myself in the relationship or was allowing myself to be manipulated. Either way, I realized I wasn't safe with that person. Instead of worrying about whether he was trustworthy, I focused my efforts on taking better care of myself with him, creating some distance from him, and, in some cases, getting the courage to end the relationship.*

We encourage you to make the same change in your own thinking. Instead of worrying about whether or not your partner really loves you or—in cases where his behavior changes radically—trying to figure out which version of him is the "real" one, ask yourself: *Can I trust myself to take care of myself with my partner?* (Your answer can really determine your next steps; we'll talk about this shortly.)

The same wise therapist corrected Beverly one day when Beverly said her mother didn't love her. "Your mother did love you," the therapist said. "She just didn't love you *enough*."

Ask yourself if the same may be true of your partner. Does he, in fact, love you—just not enough to give you the things you need and deserve in a partner?

LETTING LOVE BE YOUR MOTIVATOR

Whether or not you and your partner truly love each other makes a difference when it comes to overcoming a substance dependence and healing your relationship. The reason is this: You and your partner must work together, in collaboration, for your partner to have the best chance for recovery, and for the two of you to have a strong emotional connection. Call it love or loyalty or compassion—it is what makes that collaboration possible. Otherwise it will be too easy to discontinue your efforts when things get tough (and they will). Especially if both of you are lacking in self-love, you may need to rely on the love you have for your partner to pull you through the hard times. Love will help motivate each of you to change, even when your own self-motivation weakens.

This is no doubt contrary to what you have heard before. Most therapists and recovery experts will say that you have to be able to love yourself before you can help your partner—and in the long run, this is true. But *in the meantime*, while you are learning to love yourself and working on repairing the damage from your child-hood (or other losses), you may need to rely on the love you have for your partner to help you stay motivated to change and to help him change.

You've also likely heard that those who suffer from substance dependence need to change for themselves, not for someone else. But when you're dealing with someone who doesn't love himself—someone who, in fact, may hate himself—the only motivation he may be able to muster at first is his love for you or his children. So, again, *in the meantime*, while he is working on gaining some self-love, he may need to rely on that love for you for motivation. The good news is that the more positive changes he makes, the better he will feel about himself, and the more self-love he will develop.

Beverly: A couple of years into my relationship with the man I mentioned earlier, he and I talked about my eating habits and my excess weight. I had struggled with my weight nearly my entire life and had terrible eating habits, eating mostly the starchy, fatty foods I had been raised on. My partner assured me that he loved me the way I was, but he also told me that he was concerned about the health risks of me being overweight. Put simply, he didn't want to lose me.

At that time I lacked the internal motivation to restrict my diet or to exercise. Because I had been so deprived of love and even some of the basic necessities (including proper nutrition) as a child, I had a tremendous resistance to being deprived of food. And because I always felt awkward in my body, I hated exercise. But here I was causing my partner, a man I deeply loved, to worry, and it was that knowledge that forced me to take a good hard look at myself and decide to lose some weight—not for me, but for him.

During the time I was with him I had more motivation to eat healthy foods and to exercise than I had had in my entire life. Although it has been a life-long struggle, taking care of myself became a lot easier because of our relationship.

People who are truly in love can inspire each other to be better. When we know someone believes in us, we want to be the best we can be. We want to become worthy of their confidence in us. And this impulse can be harnessed to help both your partner and yourself.

CHAPTER 2

Do I Love My Partner Enough to Stay?

BEFORE WE GO ON, IT'S IMPORTANT THAT YOU TAKE A MOMENT to think about your partner and ask yourself: *Is there enough love left in our relationship to help heal it?*

Living with a substance-dependent partner can erode your love for him. Disappointment after disappointment, hurt after hurt can pile up until it is difficult to find the love you once shared under the rubble of broken promises, broken dreams, and broken commitments.

You may be sure that you still love your partner. When he is not using he may seem like his old self—loving, kind, caring, concerned about others. He may still be a good father, a good provider, and even a pillar of the community, volunteering his time to help others, attending church, and making a real difference in other people's lives.

But even then, you may be questioning why you are still with him. When he uses or is involved in a compulsive activity, you may witness only the selfish, egotistical, uncaring, even cruel side of him. You may find yourself wondering: *Who is the real man?*

The bottom line is this: You and you alone must be the one to decide whether you have the motivation, the strength, and the love to continue struggling with your partner one more day.

Separating your feelings of love from those of need and obligation can help you make the decision whether to stay or go. It's important to realize that you don't *need* each other. He can survive without
you, and vice versa. He doesn't need you to make him better. You
can certainly help him on his journey, and the help you offer can be
powerfully effective if you follow the strategies we recommend. But,
ultimately, he and he alone will be the one to decide to get better. If
you find you have to leave, you won't damage him to the point that
he descends into a hopeless place. (If he is that close to the edge, he
needs more help than you can offer, probably from a psychotherapist.) Don't underestimate his ability to take care of himself. Those
who are substance dependent are very resourceful.

You may be convinced that you need him as well, but this is also
far from true. No matter how dependent you have become on your
partner—financially, emotionally—you can work toward becoming
stronger and more independent.

The important thing to remember here is that needing each other
is not enough of a reason to stay together—in fact, it can add to your
relationship problems. The more you feel you need your partner, the
more angry you will be when he lets you down, and the more likely
you'll be to start a fight.

WHEN LOVING HIM IS NOT ENOUGH

Let's assume that you do feel confident that you love your partner.
You also need to feel confident that he loves you.

If your partner was sober or clean when you first met but became
addicted after, you know the toll his addiction has taken on your
relationship. You likely still remember what he was like when he was
sober and how clearly he demonstrated his love for you. And there
may be times, when he isn't using, that he still shows you how much

he loves you. The combination can make it worth it for you to stay with him and try to help him in his recovery efforts.

However, if he has been using for as long as you have known him and he's always treated you badly, he may be one of those people who are incapable of loving another person, instead using others for companionship, sex, or money.

There are other clear indications that a partner doesn't or can't love you enough to warrant your efforts to save the relationship:

- Your partner has told you that he no longer loves you.
- Your partner has told you that he no longer finds you attractive and no longer wants to have a sexual or romantic relationship with you.
- Your partner has told you that he loves someone else.
- Your partner has told you that he is gay.

It may seem obvious that if your partner has told you any of these things, you shouldn't stay in the relationship. But you may be the kind of person who needs to have things stated very bluntly before you can face the harsh truth. If your partner has told you any of these things, you should not waste your time trying to help him recover— even if *you* still love *him*. You might tell yourself that if you love him enough, or if you change enough, he will regain the love he once had for you. You might tell yourself that you love him so much that you are certain your love can heal him, and that it doesn't matter whether he loves you or not—you have love enough for both of you. You might even tell yourself that you can just be friends and still make the program laid out in this book work—that he is the father of your children or you have a business together or you have known each other for too long for you to just walk away when he needs your help.

If you are telling yourself any of these things, you are in denial. No matter how much you love him, no matter how many entanglements you have, you can't play the role of his collaborator in recovery unless there is real love between you—love that you both share. If he has moved on to another relationship, or he no longer wants to share a romantic or sexual relationship with you, or he has revealed to you that he is gay, the relationship is over and you need to move on. No matter how much you would like to help him, and no matter how much you believe you can help him, he has to want both your help *and* your love. And he has to be in a position to return that love.

IF HE HAS BECOME ABUSIVE

Even if you have good reason to believe your partner loves you (or at least as much as he is able), if he has become emotionally, physically, or sexually abusive toward you *and* he refuses to admit that he is abusive, love is not enough. We cannot stress this enough. If he tells you that he is not being abusive, that you are exaggerating and "making a mountain out of a molehill," or if he blames you for his abusive behavior ("If you didn't argue with me so much, I wouldn't hit you"), you cannot collaborate with him in his recovery from substance dependency.

The reason? An abusive relationship is not an equal one. Put simply, your partner is attempting to dominate and control you, even though he may not be aware of it consciously. He does not view you as an equal, but as someone who is beneath him, in status, intelligence, financial resources, or some other way. In order to have a collaborative relationship, you each need to see the other as an equal, not someone you can control, not someone who is your subordinate or "less than" you in some way.

Many who suffer from addiction have "co-occurring" issues, which means that they suffer not only from a substance dependence problem but also from a mental illness such as clinical depression or bipolar disorder or from a personality disorder such as narcissism or borderline personality disorder. More and more, substance abuse specialists are recognizing that they need to treat both the addiction problem and the mental illness or personality disorder, and many treatment programs now offer dual treatment. If your partner has become abusive toward you, he may need an assessment to determine whether he also has a mental illness or personality disorder.

Trauma is also highly prevalent in the history of substance abusers, including childhood trauma such as physical and sexual abuse. We will discuss this connection in more detail later on. For now, just know that if your partner has a history of childhood abuse or neglect, these experiences can lead not only to substance dependencies and compulsive behaviors but to intimate partner abuse, either emotional or physical. While it is important for you to have compassion for your partner if he had such childhood experiences, it is equally important that both of you be honest with yourselves about whether he is repeating that cycle of abuse by abusing you.

Beverly's client Robert discusses his abusive behavior toward his wife when drinking:

I hated myself because I was sexually abused as a child. I felt so much shame about it and I blamed myself for "allowing" it to happen. I drank to try to wipe out the shame, but when I got drunk I turned into a monster. All my pent-up shame and anger came out and I said horrible things to my wife—things I really felt about myself. I called her a whore and accused her of sleeping with other men. I pushed her for sex when she clearly wasn't interested, and I have to confess, sometimes I even forced myself on her sexually.

When I sobered up I felt horrible about what I had done to her. I had essentially treated her the way my perpetrator had treated me, trying to rid myself of my shame by dumping it on her. Until I became sober I refused to admit I had been abusive to her. I didn't want to face even more shame, so I lied to her and to myself about it. I denied I'd been abusive, denied I'd said those terrible things to her, denied I'd forced her into having sex.

She ended up leaving me, and I don't blame her. I wasn't ready to face my demons and I wasn't ready to admit I had been victimized by a man. I preferred to believe I had let the man have sex with me rather than admit to myself or anyone else that I had been overpowered by him. And as long as I refused to admit I had, in fact, been raped, I was a dangerous person to be around, especially when I was drinking.

If your partner is able to recognize that he has become abusive and can admit that he needs help in order to stop this behavior, it is possible to establish a collaborative relationship concerning his recovery from substance dependency. It will, however, be necessary for him to agree to go into a treatment program for those with a dual diagnosis and/or to agree to go into individual psychotherapy to work on his abuse issues. *Couples therapy is not recommended when one partner is abusive.* Not only can it be counterproductive, but often it is also damaging to the person who is being abused.

No matter how much you love your partner and he loves you, both his substance abuse issues *and* his issues surrounding abuse need to be addressed if there is any hope for a healthy relationship.

WHEN IS IT TIME TO LEAVE?

Even if you love your partner and are confident that your partner loves you, you may still decide that you can no longer live together or continue a romantic relationship. Your partner's substance dependence may have become so extreme that it is creating negative consequences not only for him, but for you as well, consequences that you simply can no longer endure.

Beverly's client Sara talks about choosing to leave her husband, whom she loved:

My husband is a wonderful man. He is a loving husband and friend to me and a great father to our son. It breaks my heart to say this, but in spite of how much I love him and he loves me, I have come to the painful conclusion that I must get a divorce from him. He is a compulsive gambler who has nearly bankrupted us.

I've tried everything to get him help so he will stop. But he is a proud man who refuses to admit he has a real problem. He refuses to go to therapy or to a twelve-step program because to him these are for "weak" people. Instead he continues to make excuses, blaming "bad luck" for his losses and continually promising to cut down on his gambling. He says it is how he copes with stress but he doesn't "need" to do it.

In order to save our house I've been advised by a lawyer that I have to get a legal separation or a divorce. That way we'll have to divide what money is left and I won't be responsible for any of his future debts or have my credit damaged.

Even though I hate to put my son through a divorce, he is getting older and soon he'll begin to understand what his father does when he goes away on weekends. And I'm afraid of the type of people my husband hangs out with. They are some pretty seedy characters. I'm afraid of what could happen to my son and myself if my husband couldn't pay a gambling debt.

If I didn't still love him so much, it wouldn't be so difficult. How do I walk away from a man who has been so good to me and my son? How do I just give up on him? I know it isn't his fault, I know some of what he went through as a child, and I know this addiction comes out of those childhood experiences, but I can't force him to get help.

Sometimes no matter how much you love each other, the problems your partner's substance abuse problems have caused are so destructive that you have to walk away. We're not talking about walking away as a form of "tough love" in order to motivate him to change. We're talking about self-preservation. When your partner's substance dependence threatens your emotional, psychological, or physical well-being, then you may have to walk away—move out, stop all contact—until he has received enough help that he's no longer a threat to you or your children.

Here are some examples of situations in which the right decision may be for you to walk away:

- Your partner has become dangerous—meaning that he presents a potential threat to the physical and/or emotional well-being of either you or your children. For example, he has become physically abusive toward you or your children, he threatens to kill you or your children, or he threatens to kill himself.

- You clearly can't take care of yourself with your partner because you allow him to continue to abuse you, betray you, or treat you poorly in other ways.

- Your partner's gambling addiction or drug abuse has put you and your children in danger. For instance, he owes money to criminals who have threatened to harm his family, or he has brought dangerous people into your life.

In these situations the question needs to shift from "Does my partner love me enough?" to "Do I love myself enough?" If you stay in your relationship despite any of the above, what you are really saying is that you do not love yourself enough to take care of yourself.

If you, too, struggle with addiction, and especially if you've been working on yourself for a long time in either a recovery program or therapy, you may need to acknowledge that you and your partner may not be at the same stage of recovery or the same level of self-awareness. This disparity may be more than you can tolerate.

As much as you love your partner and wish him well, you may not feel willing or able to wait for him to get to a place in his recovery where he can work on the relationship—or even be a decent person to be around.

One more thing to consider: Even if you decide to leave your partner, you won't be leaving behind the reasons you chose him in the first place. Unless and until you become clear about that, you are very likely to repeat the same scenario with someone else. Freud called this the "repetition compulsion," a psychological phenomenon in which a person repeats a traumatic (or highly stressful) event or its circumstances over and over again in the hopes of resolving the trauma. This includes reenacting the event or putting oneself in situations where the event is likely to happen again. In other words, you repeat the same situation with a different person hoping that, *this* time, the outcome will be different. Unfortunately, it rarely is. So if you have decided to leave your partner, make sure you still take the time you need to understand why you chose him in the first place; we will discuss possible reasons later on in the book.

Hopefully, the above information will help you decide whether to continue your relationship or end it.

If you do decide to stay, know that your belief in your partner, yourself, and your relationship can help get you through the hard times. It won't be easy. It is going to take hard work and impeccable self-honesty on your part. And you're going to have to learn a lot about self-care, limits, and boundaries.

But if you choose to go forward, welcome. We will try to help you feel good about your decision all along the way. Remember, you are not doing this just for your partner, you are doing it for yourself as well. Chances are you are going to help yourself as much as you are helping him.

CHAPTER 3

Hope and Compassion: The Keys to Healing

"Compassion will cure more sins than condemnation."
—HENRY WARD BEECHER

IF YOU STILL FEEL LOVE TOWARD YOUR PARTNER AND YOU STILL have hope that he can change, we have good news for you: A great deal of new research shows that recovery from substance abuse is much more feasible than ever before. We learn more every day about what causes addiction, why it is so difficult to manage, and how best to treat it. We now know that a person doesn't need to "hit bottom" before he can begin to change. And we know that there are many treatment options in addition to twelve-step and residential programs.

In the area of neuroscience alone, major breakthroughs offer those with substance abuse problems a great deal of hope. Specifically, we now know that our brains are constantly evolving. Our brains don't grow only in our formative years; they create new pathways long into adulthood. What this means is that given help and time and sometimes medication, plus concerted effort and measures to safeguard against returning to substance use, substance abusers can develop new patterns of behavior. And those with drug dependencies can heal their brains.

If your partner is already in recovery in some form, you have even more reason to feel hopeful. Even if he has relapsed many times, the fact that he has admitted he has a problem and has reached out for help is half the battle. Most experts now understand that relapse is actually a natural part of recovery.

Even more good news? We've learned that you can play an important role in your partner's recovery. Relationships between substance-dependent individuals and their partners are typically considered not only painful but also destructive, for both parties. But this doesn't have to be the case. There is another way for these couples to relate to one another—one that allows them to tap into their love for each other, as well as helping them bypass the obstacles that can get in the way of that love.

THE OLD WAY OF THINKING

Until recently, traditional methods of treatment for substance problems viewed a person's motivation to change in black and white terms: Either he was ready to change or he was not. People who seemingly didn't have the motivation to change were told to come back when they were "ready." Family members were told to "disengage" since there was nothing they could do until their loved one was ready. You may have been told that the best way to help your substance dependent partner is *not* to help. Especially if you are someone who exhibits codependent behavior, you have likely been told to "detach with love" or to practice "tough love." Often those who have read books on codependency worry about doing anything nice for their partner for fear of "enabling" his destructive behavior.

"I call that an 'action stopping' myth," says Debra Jay, interventionist, lecturer, and coauthor with her husband, Jeff Jay, of the book *Love First: A Family's Guide to Intervention.* "It says you can't help an alcoholic until he wants help. So that's it for families: Step back and let the addiction run through your family like a freight train. There's nothing you can do. And we hear that all the time. We hear it from doctors; we hear it from people in Alcoholics Anonymous. It just stops people from thinking about it."

This view leaves clinicians as well as family members with only two options: passively wait for the person to gain that motivation on their own, or aggressively demand change, often through confrontation.

But today's experts are turning this idea on its head. "It's a completely different story when you say, 'If you can't help an alcoholic until he wants help, what will get him to want help?'" Jay points out. "You see, now I'm thinking differently. Now that opens up the door to possibility. Now I can start looking for solutions and answers."[1]

CRAFT: A NEW APPROACH FOR CHANGE

Thanks to new research, we now know that family members and others important to a substance abuser can have a positive impact on his motivation. Specifically, Community Reinforcement and Family Training (CRAFT) is a scientifically supported, evidence-based approach to helping families of substance abusers, one that we draw from for our suggestions here.

CRAFT grew out of treatment innovations that began in the 1970s. A group of researchers in Illinois, led by behavioral psychologist Nathan Azrin, developed what is considered the most effective behavioral treatment for substance users—the Community Reinforcement Approach (CRA). In the process, they discovered that *family involvement was a crucial factor in successful change.* Dr. Robert J. Meyers (one of the original Illinois group) expanded the CRA approach to work with families when their loved one refused help, and called it CRAFT. After moving to the Center on Alcoholism,

Substance Abuse, and Addictions (CASAA) at the University of New Mexico, Meyers conducted further research and clinical trials (teaming with Dr. Jane Ellen Smith). Their work has now provided ample evidence that given the right tools, family can effect change.

CRAFT is designed specifically to empower family members. It teaches them how to take control of their lives and to change their interactions with the substance abuser in ways that promote positive behavioral change. Clinical trials have shown that when family members use CRAFT's positive, supportive, nonconfrontational techniques, including those we offer in this book, not only do they find ways to get their loved one into treatment, but the family members themselves feel better—specifically, they show decreases in depression, anger, and anxiety. Clinical trials have also suggested that family members benefit emotionally even if their loved one does not enter treatment.[2]

Research groups that studied the CRAFT program observed two results:

- Two-thirds of substance users who had initially been resistant to treatment agreed to treatment.

- The majority of participating spouses and parents reported being happier, less depressed, and less angry, and having more family cohesion and less family conflict than prior to their CRAFT sessions, *whether or not their loved one engaged in treatment.*

Both results were found across substance and relationship types, and held true for all socioeconomic, ethnic, and age groups.

CRAFT shows us that while you can't change your addicted partner, you can change yourself in ways that will benefit your partner and your relationship with him, and greatly improve his chances of recovery. We will share with you some of CRAFT's strategies for doing so, as well as some of our own.

Like the CRAFT program, our approach draws its strength from collaboration and compassion rather than confrontation and conflict. This is the core of our approach.

COMPASSION AS KEY TO HEALING

Throughout this book we will be offering you a lot of helpful information and many strategies to support your partner on his healing journey, based on our experience and expertise, on the expertise of other professionals in the field of recovery, and on the latest research. But the most important information we will offer in this entire book is this: Compassion is the most powerful tool you can have when it comes to healing addictions of any kind. Put simply, what your partner needs the most from you is *compassion*.

Compassion for others is deeply rooted in human nature; it has a biological basis in the brain and body. It seems that we are wired to respond to others in need. As part of a research project conducted by Emory University neuroscientists James Rilling and Gregory Berns, participants were given the chance to help someone else while their brain activity was recorded. What they found was that helping others triggers activity in the caudate nucleus and anterior cingulate, portions of the brain that turn on when people receive rewards or experience pleasure. In other words, helping others brings the same pleasure we get from gratifying personal desire.

The reaction of another bodily system (the nervous system) also suggests a biological basis for compassion. Our nervous systems play a role in regulating our blood flow and breathing patterns; when we feel threatened, our hearts and breathing rates usually increase, preparing us to either confront or flee from the threat. But when we feel compassion for others, our heart rates slow down, preparing us not to fight or flee, but to approach and soothe. In other words, the science tells us that having compassion for others is actually good for us.

In the last thirty years the science of psychology and studies of the human brain have put compassion, caring, and other prosocial behavior center stage in the development of our well-being and mental health. Most recently, the work of many researchers has revealed that kindness, support, encouragement, and compassion from others have a huge impact on how our brains and bodies develop and function. Love and kindness, especially in early life, even affect how some of our genes are expressed.[3]

Compassion is especially effective when it comes to healing shame, which as we've seen is closely connected to addiction. Most, perhaps all, people who have a substance abuse problem feel deep shame, stemming either from events in their childhood or from the reactions (their own as well as others') to their addictive behavior, and often both. Compassion is, as it turns out, the only antidote to shame—the only thing that can counteract and neutralize shame's isolating, stigmatizing, debilitating poison.

The word *compassion* comes from the Latin roots *com* (with) and *pati* (suffer). When we offer someone genuine compassion, we "suffer with" them—that is, we join them in their suffering. And in doing so, we provide the person with not one, but five healing gifts:

1. We let them know that we really *see them*—that we recognize their suffering. One of the most powerful needs for humans is to *be seen*. This is especially true for those with a substance abuse problem who were also victims of childhood neglect and abuse and who often felt invisible within their families.

2. We let them know that we *hear them*. Being heard is another primal need for humans and, again, one that often went unmet early on for those with substance abuse issues.

3. We *validate them* and their experience—we let them know that we recognize their suffering and their right to express their pain, sadness, fear, anger, or any other emotion due to that suffering. We don't deny, minimize, or ignore that suffering, which is what those with substance abuse issues may have grown accustomed to as a child (and so may continue to expect).

4. We let them know that we *care about them* as human beings—that we care about the fact that they suffered and are still suffering. Respect and care for the substance abuser's humanity may have been in short supply when he was a child, and it is a gift to have this birthright restored.

5. We *comfort them,* whether with kind words, a healing glance, a loving touch, or a supportive hug. The gift of comfort stimulates the soothing/contentment system in the body and provides a sense of security that helps tone down negative emotions.

So, as you endeavor to support your partner in his healing journey, we encourage you to be kind and patient and loving and compassionate. Far from enabling your partner, acting in these ways is the key to helping him. Being compassionate doesn't mean condoning or supporting the behavior you don't want. But it does mean, just as a start, revising the way you think about addiction.

PART II.

TAKING ON A COMPASSIONATE ATTITUDE

CHAPTER 4

A Fresh Look at Addiction

*"There is always loss of self before addiction starts,
either from trauma or childhood emotional loss."*
—Dr. Gabor Maté, *In the Realm of Hungry
Ghosts: Close Encounters with Addiction*

THE MORE YOU KNOW ABOUT ADDICTION AND ABOUT YOUR
partner's particular situation, the more empathy you will gain for what
he is going through, which will set the stage for true compassion.
That's why, in this chapter, we are presenting a program designed to
help you take a second look at some of your preconceived ideas about
addiction and about people who are substance dependent, as well as
help you better understand your partner.

This program has six steps:

1. Take on a new attitude.

2. Use new language.

3. Normalize the situation.

4. Assume your partner has a reason for using.

5. Learn more about substance dependency.

6. Adopt a trauma-sensitive approach.

Of course, everyone is different. The information we share with you here is based on what is generally true for many or most addicts, but please remember that it may not fit all situations.

STEP 1: TAKING ON A NEW ATTITUDE

Our culture tends to take a very negative view of people who suffer from an addiction. We often see them as selfish, even narcissistic people who are incapable of putting their needs aside in order to recognize the needs of others—people who are so self-centered that they don't see how much they are hurting those they love. Or we see them as weak-willed and self-indulgent, without the self-discipline or self-respect to stop their negative behaviors.

But these characterizations are seldom accurate. Those who are addicted often feel a great deal of shame about the fact that they are hurting their loved ones. And it has been proven over and over that those who suffer from addictions are not weak-willed or self-indulgent but, rather, strong people who have survived horrendous abuse, neglect, loss, abandonment, disappointment, or other trauma that many others could not have survived. Far from being weak-willed, they have been able to will themselves to go on with life in spite of their hardships.

But however strong their will, their addiction has proven to be stronger—or, more accurately, the reasons why they are addicted are so powerful that until these reasons are brought out into the open and the accompanying needs are addressed, the addicted person is unable to stop their addictive behavior. Their "self-indulgence" is actually a way for them to self-medicate and self-soothe so they can endure the pain and shame they feel every day.

Many of the experts Chris interviewed for his book *Recover to Live* made observations about the contributions to society that highly functional substance or activity dependent people have made and continue to make. For example, Dr. Drew Pinsky, addiction medicine specialist and clinical professor at the USC School of Medicine, said that it pains him "that addicts are perceived as weak or bad. Because one of the reasons I work with addicts is that they're one of the most powerful, richest, most human groups of people you could ever meet."[4]

Many with substance or activity dependencies are extremely intelligent and talented people who have contributed great things to our culture. Famous artists, writers, actors, and musicians who have suffered from an alcohol or drug dependency include Vincent van Gogh, Jackson Pollock, Ernest Hemingway, Charles Dickens, Robert Louis Stevenson, F. Scott Fitzgerald, Dylan Thomas, James Thurber, Tennessee Williams, Edgar Allan Poe, Stephen King, Richard Burton, Anthony Hopkins, Orson Welles, Judy Garland, Robin Williams, Billie Holiday, Frank Sinatra, Stevie Ray Vaughan, Eric Clapton, and Steven Tyler.

As Kristen Johnston, actress and author of the book *Guts: The Endless Follies and Tiny Triumphs of a Giant Disaster,* so eloquently stated: "A huge number of the recovering drug addicts I know seem to have a few things in common, other than their disease: intelligence, creativity, individualism, humor, and . . . enormous amounts of ambition."

Research has shown no evidence to support the idea that there is a "type" of person who becomes an addict or that there is a set of "addictive personality" traits (such as dishonesty, self-centeredness, weak will, laziness, or a broken moral compass). Yet our culture lumps all addicts together, despite the evidence that people come to their substance problems for all sorts of reasons.[5]

Simply understanding and believing this can lead to a major shift in your attitude toward your partner, and with it the way you treat him. Let's use the idea that all addicts are dishonest as an example.

Dishonesty is an almost inevitable part of managing compulsions. Think of it this way: It is very difficult to meet the demands of daily living (job responsibilities, family, and other relationships) while at the same time meeting the demands associated with compulsive behaviors (finding the time to indulge the behavior, covering up signs of using). Something has to give, and most often that something is being truthful.

Understanding the all too human reasons your partner may lie to you (or let you believe a partial truth, or tell you what he thinks you want to hear) can help bridge broken trust and encourage more honesty. The next time you catch your partner in a lie, instead of blowing up or telling yourself this is further proof that he doesn't love you, ask yourself: Is it possible that he is . . .

- afraid of real-world consequences (job loss, relationship loss)?
- afraid you will be disappointed in him?
- afraid you will think he is weak?
- afraid and overwhelmed by the idea of change?
- afraid he can't change?
- afraid of being a failure?

Rather than simply branding your partner as a liar, look more closely at when he lies, and see if you can understand why. Does he lie mostly to cover up his substance or activity dependence? If the dishonesty does not spill over into other parts of your partner's life—and if he feels remorse for his dishonesty—then the behavior is within the range of normal for a person with substance problems.[6] He may not be fundamentally dishonest, but rather uses dishonesty to try to avoid being shamed.

None of this means that you have to like (or even pretend to like) your partner's dishonesty, or that there shouldn't be consequences for it. But understanding why your partner lies can help you stay calm enough to use the communication skills you'll learn in this book, and increase compassion toward him, both of which should help him become increasingly honest with you.

Research has shown that the more you criticize someone, even in an attempt to "get through" to him, the more defensive he will become. On the other hand, the more your attitude changes, the more loved and accepted he will feel, and the less need he will have to defend himself or make excuses for his behavior. He'll have less of a need to lie to you or push you away with criticisms of his own.

STEP 2: USING NEW LANGUAGE

The second step in developing a compassionate attitude toward those who are substance or activity dependent is to pay attention to our language. We can start by not calling them "addicts." As Chris notes in *Recover to Live*, it is important to use language that is both sensitive and clear.

Labeling has been found to have a demonstrated negative impact both on the person who suffers from the addiction and on how others view and treat him. A label like "addict" is loaded with negative associations that can affect how we feel about the person, how we treat him, and how he feels about himself and his ability to change. Even in settings designed to treat substance problems, a survey of counselors found that they identified the term "addict" with lying, irresponsibility, and denial.[7]

Not only are labels stigmatizing, but they often don't adequately describe the person or the situation. As we've discussed, one description does not fit all when it comes to addiction, and there is no evidence to suggest that there is a specific type of person who becomes an "addict." Even professional counselors have begun to refer not to "addicts" but to "people having problems with substances."

So for the most part, from this point forward in this book, we will substitute the word *dependency* for the word *addiction* wherever possible, and use phrases like "substance dependency" or "substance problems" when we refer to those who are addicted. For clarification we will refer to those who are dependent on a substance (such as alcohol, drugs, or food) as being "substance dependent" and those who are dependent on an activity (such as work, sex, gambling, or shopping) as being "activity dependent." We suggest you pay close attention to the language you use when referring to your partner and his substance dependency problem, too!

STEP 3: NORMALIZING THE SITUATION

One of the best ways to change our negative perceptions and beliefs about those who are substance dependent or activity dependent is to recognize just how many people we are talking about. We are not talking about a minority of people, but millions and millions of them.

According to the authors of *Beyond Addiction: How Science and Kindness Help People Change,* some 22.2 million Americans, or nearly one in twelve, have substance problems severe enough to be classified as dependence or abuse. Over 30 percent of American adults abuse alcohol at some point in their lives.[8]

According to well-documented statistics for the United States, when we break it down into categories the numbers are even higher, as Chris notes in *What Addicts Know:*[9]

- 17 million with alcoholism
- 19.9 million who abuse drugs
- 4 million with eating disorders

- 10 million with gambling problems
- 12 million with sexual compulsions
- 43 million who smoke cigarettes

To complete the picture, let's add those in recovery from a substance problem. According to the results of a 2012 survey by the Partnership for Drug-Free Kids at DrugFree.org, at least 10 percent of American adults aged eighteen and older are recovering from drug and alcohol abuse. If we add those people who are recovering from sexual compulsions, gambling problems, smoking, and food-related issues we are looking at about *one in five of all adults—maybe even one in four.*

This figure is particularly interesting when we look at the rate of childhood abuse. It is estimated that one in three girls and one in four boys worldwide are sexually abused, and that one in three girls will be sexually abused, raped, and/or beaten in her lifetime. We discuss childhood abuse and trauma as key factors in developing addictions below.

Looking at the statistics, it becomes evident that it is not just weak, immature, self-centered, or indulgent people who suffer from substance dependency. It is a huge number of "normal" people, as well.

It used to be that when we thought about or talked about drug dependency, we were referring to young people, people in the inner city, people of color, and perhaps musicians, actors, and artists. But the profile of drug dependency has changed. Today, people from upper- and middle-class backgrounds, educated people with careers and families, are becoming heroin addicts or dependent on drugs like OxyContin. High school students are graduating from marijuana to cocaine to heroin in a matter of months. Middle-aged women are becoming addicted to prescription drugs after suffering an accident and needing painkillers.

Anyone can develop a substance or activity dependence. While many people who become dependent have a history of abuse or neglect, this is not true for everyone. We often think of those with dependency problems as coming from chaotic, alcoholic, or otherwise troubled households, but this is not always the case.

Recently, a very unlikely group of people have been found to suffer from prescription and other drug dependency—Mormons. Drug dependence has become an epidemic in Utah, a primarily Mormon state. People who grew up in a family where they were taught to never smoke or drink, much less take drugs; people who were raised to value the body and think of it as a temple; and people who grew up in affluent homes with strong family support are now among those who have a drug dependence.

One reason for the increasing numbers of people with substance dependency is that we have created an environment and a culture in which we are cut off from others and ourselves. The rise of addiction can be seen as a symptom of a deeper sickness in the way we live. As Chris wrote in his book *What Addicts Know*: "As a culture we've become addicted not only to gambling, drugs, alcohol, and the other usual suspects, but also to technology, the acquisition of material possessions, and every conceivable promise of instant gratification. We eat more, spend more, take more risks, and abuse more substances . . . only to feel more depressed, unsatisfied, discontent, and unhappy."[10]

We are constantly striving for more—more "things," more stimulation, more success or public recognition. What we are left with is what Chris calls "the throbbing emptiness" that sets in when we realize that these things do not fulfill us.

When we view substance dependence as a symptom of being disconnected from ourselves and from others, and realize that we all suffer from this same problem, we see that our partner is not so different from us, and our compassion increases.

STEP 4: ASSUMING YOUR PARTNER HAS A REASON FOR USING

The mental health and substance abuse treatment communities have only recently come to realize what those who work with victims and abusers have known for many years—namely, that those who suffer from substance abuse were usually traumatized in childhood. Your partner is likely no different.

The most common form of trauma is childhood abuse or neglect, but it can also include suffering the loss of a parent or other loved one, being abandoned, or being severely bullied by peers.

Negative self-concepts that develop as a result of traumas such as childhood abuse have the potential to persist throughout one's lifespan. Many adult survivors of childhood abuse engage in unhealthy coping strategies, such as problematic alcohol use, in an attempt to lessen their lasting experience of distress and/or negative self-appraisals.[11]

According to Miles Adcox, CEO of Onsite Workshops in Tennessee, a treatment center devoted to therapeutic trauma and compulsivity programs: "You can say that all self-defeating, self-destructive, persistent, resistant-to-change behavior is rooted in trauma—trauma that was most likely born out of a family system." He adds, "I actually see this a little stronger in the process addictions, such as gambling."[12]

> **Chris:** *How do you define trauma? A case can be made that simply being human is traumatic, no matter what life circumstances you were born into. If you were blessed to be delivered into a loving environment, you have a much better chance of not being seriously traumatized by this world. Few of us are so lucky, unfortunately. And all the cumulative traumas we absorb early in life, whatever form those traumas take, influence how we relate to other people.*

My parents carried the genetics of addiction, which always makes the giving of unconditional love more challenging. I grew up in a culture of power, sex, and control. The men were tolerated—even celebrated—in pursuing whatever they wanted, simply because they were powerful and attractive. They engaged in a permissiveness and selfishness that today I could not and would not choose to live with.

I was eight years old when I first experienced trauma in an overt way, in the form of public violence. The culture of chemical and behavioral addiction I was growing up in went from a future handicap in my efforts to establish healthy, loving relationships to game over. I was in a Catholic grade school class on November 22, 1963, when the nuns came to get me and told me that the president—my Uncle Jack—had been shot. In an instant my life went from light to dark. The murder of my uncle led to the breakup of my parents' marriage, a move cross-country, an absent father, and an emotionally devastated mother. It was confusing and terrifying.

Then, when I was thirteen, it happened again. On June 5, 1968, I came down for breakfast and was told by the woman who took care of my sisters and me that my Uncle Bobby had been assassinated. My mother was in California working with her brother on his presidential campaign. This time, there would be no glimmer of hope that we would survive the pain of it all. What was lost that day for our family and our generation was not just the man, but also the belief that bold men with new ideas could make a difference and change the world for the better. We tried as a family to believe in the ethic that one person can make a difference and that all of us should try, but the violence diminished us. We persevered—through force of will, self-medication, and never breathing a word about what had happened—but the trauma devastated everyone.

My mother became emotionally unreliable from those days forward. I wanted to help her but couldn't. She tried to be there for me as my own addictions flourished but couldn't.

As for my father, Peter Lawford, he would show up in New York and take us out to dinner a couple times a year. He attempted to bond with me later, when I was in my early twenties, but the effort was haphazard and more detrimental than if he had not tried at all. He was dying from his own addictions and wounds and couldn't see anything wrong with bringing his only son along for the ride. He didn't know how to be a father and he no longer had the will or capacity to learn.

The murders of my uncles spread posttraumatic stress disorder throughout my entire family—none of us were spared—and that trauma reoccurs to this day. Unaware people continue to bring up the subject of my uncles' deaths with Kennedy family members, as if the trauma no longer affects us. In 2013, fifty years after the murder of President Kennedy, a woman came up to me and began giving me her take on one of the many conspiracy theories behind the murder of my uncle. Though I didn't even acknowledge my PTSD until about five years ago, I am now acutely aware how this sort of psychic damage often remains undiagnosed, even when it's expressed as active addiction.

I recognize now that my trauma contributed significantly to my embrace of drug addiction as a way to cope. Being aware of this brings some understanding to those lost decades of my life, along with the awareness that the drugs I took might have actually saved my life. I am not sure that I would have made it without chemicals to take the edge off the pain, if only temporarily. That awareness fortifies me in my recovery, sustains me when the going gets tough, and, most of all, allows me to have compassion for myself.

THE CONNECTION BETWEEN ABUSE AND SHAME

As a counselor, Beverly has specialized for thirty-five years in working with adults who were abused as children. Most of her clients suffer from *debilitating shame*: shame so all-consuming that it negatively affects every aspect of a person's life—his perception of himself, his relationships with others, his ability to be intimate with a romantic partner, his ability to risk and achieve success in his career, and his overall physical and emotional health. While everyone experiences shame from time to time, and many have issues related to shame, adult victims of childhood abuse suffer from shame more often and have far more issues related to shame than any other group of people.

Victims of childhood abuse tend to feel shame because, as human beings, we want to believe that we have control over what happens to us. When that belief is challenged by a victimization of any kind, we feel humiliated. We imagine that we should have been able to defend ourselves. And because we weren't able to do so, we feel helpless and powerless. This powerlessness leads to humiliation and shame.

While all victims feel the humiliation connected with powerlessness, men tend to feel it even more than women since even as young boys, they internalize the cultural expectation that they should be tough and strong and that weakness is frowned upon.

It is especially shaming to a child when a parent abuses him, violating his body and integrity. Because parental love is so important, children will make up all kinds of excuses for a parent's behavior—even abusive behavior. Most often the child ends up blaming himself for "causing" his parent to abuse him, which protects him from facing the truth about his parents' abuse but at the same time locks him into a pattern of self-blame.

The more you can learn about your partner's childhood, and the clearer a connection you can draw between his history and why he uses, the easier it may be for you to treat him with compassion. But simply reminding yourself that there is a reason behind your partner's addiction, even if that reason is not immediately apparent to you, can help you feel more compassionate toward him.

Beverly's client Wendy came to see her about her husband's workaholism. Here's how she described the situation:

> My husband works ten to twelve hours a day and often works on weekends. Even when he is at home he is constantly answering the phone or working on the computer. He has essentially become a stranger to me and the kids. For years now he has promised to spend more time at home, but I can see that he is never going to change. I've tried nagging, blackmailing, threatening, trying to make him feel guilty . . . but nothing works. I stayed with him for the kids but now I realize they don't really have a father anyway. I've come to therapy as a last resort. I need to know that I've done everything possible to save my marriage.

Beverly explained to Wendy that the first step was for her to understand all she could about her husband's activity dependence. Beverly assumed that, like all substance dependent people, Craig was "addicted" to work because it provided him some kind of reward and because it helped him run away from or cope with his pain or shame. She explained these two concepts to Wendy and gave her a homework assignment.

The first part of the assignment was for her to write about the reasons why her husband might be feeling pain or shame, and in particular about any trauma or abuse he might have experienced in his childhood. The second part was for her to write about the rewards she imagined her husband received from his excessive working behavior.

The next week, Wendy showed an immediate change in her attitude: "I always knew Craig had a rough childhood—he'd talked about it at the beginning of our relationship. But somehow I had forgotten about it." She explained:

His mother was a very domineering and critical woman. She criticized Craig for not getting good enough grades in school and for not being popular enough. And she complained constantly about Craig's father not making enough money. Craig often overheard her telling his father that she had made a mistake to marry such a loser—that she could have had her pick of men who would have made a lot more money. Craig had told me that he thought his father was a wimp to put up with that kind of treatment from his mother. But he had also told me that her complaints about him and his father had motivated him to try harder—that in a way her high expectations had made him want to be a success.

The connection is so clear to me now. Craig has been working so hard because he didn't want to be like his father—a failure. And in a weird way, he is still trying to impress his mother. Every time he sees her he brags about how well his business is doing. And he's constantly buying her things—a new appliance, even a new car. It's like he's buying her love. Poor guy.

Beverly asked Wendy if she was now willing to help Craig with his dependence on work:

Yes, for the first time in a long time I don't feel angry with him. And I'm not taking his constant working personally. For so long I assumed he just didn't want to be around me. Now I realize he had completely different reasons for his behavior.

Wendy's realizations allowed her to understand that when she shamed Craig for working long hours, she was unwittingly repeating his mother's behavior—something she never wanted to do. Instead, Beverly suggested that when Craig came home late Wendy could say something like, "You look exhausted. Is there anything I can do to help you feel better?" and that when he came home at a decent hour, Wendy could give him a big hug and say something like, "I'm so glad you're home. I love having you here in the evenings." (We'll discuss this rewarding type of behavior in later chapters.)

{EXERCISE}

REASONS AND REWARDS

1. Write about why you think your partner may be feeling pain or shame. In particular, remember what he has
   told you about his childhood or what you have learned
   from being around his family. Make sure you include any
   traumatic events your partner experienced such as child
   abuse, abandonment, loss of a parent, and so on.
2. Now write about the rewards your partner may gain from
   relying on a substance or activity.

STEP 5: LEARNING MORE ABOUT SUBSTANCE DEPENDENCY

The fifth step to developing a new attitude toward your partner is to learn more about substance dependency, including where it comes from and how it works.

While there are no easy answers, we now know that addiction is the result of a complex interaction of multiple factors. These include a person's genetic and psychological makeup and experience, developmental and social history, and even the expectations of the culture in which he lives.[13]

The Role of the Brain in Dependency Problems

Some of the most recent discoveries in the science of addiction have focused on a neurotransmitter called dopamine. Dopamine is concentrated in the brain's reward system and pleasure centers—the areas most impacted by substance use and compulsive behaviors. Thanks to a combination of genetics and environment, some people's brains generate more dopamine than others; those people have the capacity to enjoy a larger range of experiences than others.

Dopamine is what makes us feel good. It is naturally generated through ordinary, pleasurable activities like eating and having sex, and it is the brain's way of rewarding us for activities necessary for our survival. It focuses our attention on the cues that surrounded whatever thing or activity made us feel good. (These cues eventually become triggers, as will be explained in chapter 10.)[14]

Drugs and alcohol (and certain behaviors) turn on a flood of dopamine in the brain; as a result, we feel good, even euphoric. But dopamine produced by these artificial means immediately throws our pleasure and reward systems out of whack. Flooding the brain repeatedly with dopamine has a dangerous long-term effect: It creates what is referred to as *tolerance,* a state in which we lose our ability to produce or absorb dopamine and therefore need more and more of it artificially just to feel okay. In short, the brain is forced to compensate for artificially high levels of dopamine by decreasing its own production of it or by reducing the number of dopamine receptors (thus desensitizing itself)—or both.[15]

A lowered level of dopamine is a big part of what creates "cravings"—physiological drives to regain the normal dopamine balance of the brain. The strength of these cravings can lead a person to continue using a substance even when he is experiencing negative consequences and despite a strong desire to change. Depending on the length of time and quantities the person has been using, their cravings can be extremely uncomfortable and powerful.[16]

The dopamine system will begin to recover as soon as it's no longer being flooded, but it takes time, and people tend to feel worse before they feel better. Their brains are telling them that by stopping using, something is wrong—no matter how well intentioned they are or how much effort they put into recovery. This is a huge factor in relapse. (Knowing this can help you and your partner make it through this recovery period. Medication and behavioral strategies can also help, as we will discuss in coming chapters.)

Dopamine balance is not the only thing that is affected by repeated substance use. Activity in key structures in the brain, such as the prefrontal cortex and limbic system, is also disrupted. The prefrontal cortex is the part of the brain where we assess risks, weigh consequences, and make plans. It acts as a "braking system," making possible the judgments and decisions that help us rein in our impulses. When flooded with a substance, such as alcohol or drugs, this part of the brain basically shuts down. The limbic system is responsible for emotions and basic drives; it's where our desires and sense of urgency come from. Under the influence of a substance or compulsive behavior, this part of the brain gets excited into overdrive. And like the cravings that arise from low levels of dopamine, "the runaway limbic system is also an automatic, physiological process that is outside conscious control."[17]

With the prefrontal cortex shut down and the limbic system overexcited, someone with substance dependencies is very likely to go forward with the impulse to use. "A brain in this state will register the smell of marijuana being smoked, the desire to smoke it, and anticipate the feeling that comes along with smoking it, while the reasons not to smoke it disappear."[18]

Knowing all this—understanding why it's so difficult, biologically, for your partner to stop using—can make it easier to be compassionate toward him as he attempts to do so. And the latest research can also give you hope: Scientists in the exciting field of interpersonal neurobiology are proving that other people can affect us all the way down to a molecular level. Our brains are changed by our relationships, which means that you can compete with the physiological effects drugs have on your partner. Your love, empathy, encouragement, and limits have strong physiological effects, too.

Isolation as a Factor in Drug Dependence

For years it was believed that drugs like cocaine and heroin are biologically addictive, meaning that anyone who took them for a period of, say, twenty-one days was highly likely to become an addict. This belief came in part from rat experiments in which a rat, put into a cage with two water bottles—one containing only water, the other laced with heroin or cocaine—almost always became obsessed with the drugged water and kept coming back for more and more until it killed itself.

But in the 1970s, Bruce Alexander, a professor of psychology in Vancouver, noticed something about these experiments: The rats were put in cages alone, with nothing to do but take the drugs. What would happen, he wondered, if that weren't the case? He built Rat Park, a lush cage in which the rats had colored balls and the best rat food and tunnels to scamper down, plus plenty of other rats to interact with. And then he ran the experiment again, isolating some test subjects while putting others together in his newly built cage.

All the rats tried both water bottles, but what happened next was startling. The rats who lived in Rat Park didn't like the drugged water. They mostly shunned it, consuming less than a quarter of the drugs that the isolated rats used, and none of them died. All the isolated rats became heavy users, but none of the Rat Park rats did.

Just in case you doubt the implications of the Rat Park experiments for humans, consider the case of heroin use in the military during the Vietnam War. According to a study published in the *Archives of General Psychiatry,* some 20 percent of US soldiers became addicted to heroin while in Vietnam because it was reported to be as common as chewing gum. Many people were understandably worried that a huge number of soldiers would return home as addicts. But, in fact, according to the same study, some 95 percent of the addicted soldiers simply stopped using once they returned home.

Alexander maintains that this discovery is a profound challenge to both the view that addiction is a moral failing and the view that addiction is a disease of a chemically hijacked brain. He argues, instead, that addiction is an adaptation. In other words, the reason your partner is addicted is not him, it's his cage.

Alexander took his rat experiments further to investigate whether those who develop addictions have their brains hijacked to the point that they can't recover. He reran the early experiments where the rats were left alone, and let the rats use for fifty-seven days. Then he took them out of isolation and placed them in Rat Park. What happened was striking. The rats seemed to have a few twitches of withdrawal but soon stopped their heavy use and went back to a normal life. The Rat Park habitat saved them.

People are frequently given diamorphine, the medical name for heroin, for pain relief when they are hospitalized for an injury. The heroin patients receive in hospitals is purer and more potent than the heroin used by street addicts. If drug addiction is caused by drugs, then we should find that many people leave the hospital addicted to heroin. But it virtually never happens. Typically, medical users just stop, despite sometimes months of use. So, why does the same drug, used for the same length of time, turn street users into desperate addicts? The street addict is likely similar to the rats in those first experiments—isolated, and with only one source of solace: the drug. Many medical patients are like the rats in Rat Park. They go home to a life where they are surrounded by people who they love and who love them. The drug is the same, but the environment is different. (As far as we know, there has been no follow-up research to discover what happens to medical patients who don't go home to people who love them—whether they are more inclined to become addicted.)

The story we have been told—that the cause of addiction is chemical—isn't false. But what is emerging from the latest addiction research is that the human need for connection is at least as important. Human beings have a deep need to bond and form connections. If we can't connect with each other, we will connect with whatever we can find. In other words, *it is disconnection that drives addiction.* A heroin addict bonds with heroin because he can't bond as fully with anyone or anything else.[19]

Chris shared his experience of the connection between isolation and his drinking and drug dependence in *Recover to Live:*

> This disease is so much about feeling isolated and believing that you're the only person with this issue. Because of my family upbringing, I had a lot of rationalizations around being different: *Nobody is like me. I am special. My situation is unique.*
>
> But when you walk into a room full of strangers and open yourself up, just for a little bit, you see that everybody is really just like you. I went into my first [12-Step recovery] meeting and a guy was telling what sounded like my story . . . and in that moment of mutual identification our connection obliterated my sense of uniqueness.[20]

So it is important to remember another reason why compassion is so crucial: It can reduce your partner's feelings of isolation. And understanding isolation's role in addiction can help you remember not to respond to your partner's behavior in ways that exacerbate those feelings.

The Role of Genes, the Family, and Abuse in Substance Dependence

For many years now, scientists have argued that addictions such as alcoholism are strongly influenced by genetics. In fact, some have stated unequivocally that the single most reliable indicator of risk for future alcohol and drug problems is family history.

According to the National Institute on Alcohol Abuse and Alcoholism (NIAA), many scientific studies, including research conducted with twins and children of alcoholics, have demonstrated that genetic factors influence alcoholism. Children of alcoholics are about four times more likely than the general population to develop alcohol dependence problems. Children of alcoholics also have a higher risk of developing many other behavioral problems.

However, scientists have not found an "addiction gene." They have found evidence of different genetic vulnerabilities, but the relationship between genes and behavior, between what we inherit and what we do, is complicated. *Heritability* refers to how much genetic factors account for a person's risk of an illness or disorder, relative to another person's. The heritability of addictions ranges from 40 to 70 percent, depending upon the substance. These rates are in line with those of mood, anxiety, and other disorders that are considered moderately genetically driven.[21]

Even alcoholism, which is considered more heavily influenced by genetics than other addictions, is not determined only by one's genes. Indeed, more than half of all children of alcoholics do not become alcoholics themselves. The research shows that many factors influence one's risk. Environmental and social factors such as childhood neglect or abuse, trauma, loss of a parent as a child, and poor parent-child relationships have been found to predict substance problems, as has starting use early in life. And genes are not the only things that children inherit from their parents. Children are also influenced by how their parents behave—how they treat each other and their children—and these aspects of family life also affect the risk for alcoholism. In particular, researchers believe that certain family circumstances can increase a person's risk:

- An alcoholic parent is depressed or has other psychological problems.

- Both parents abuse alcohol and other drugs.
- The parents' alcohol abuse is severe.
- Conflicts lead to aggression and violence in the family.

An even stronger risk factor for alcoholism than these, however, is childhood physical or sexual abuse. Childhood abuse is linked to a variety of maladaptive outcomes that can extend into adulthood, including both internalizing disorders (depression, anxiety, suicidal ideation) and externalizing problems (conduct disorders, aggression, inappropriate or early sexual behavior), but alcohol use disorders are one of the most significant. In fact, the connection between childhood abuse and alcohol use disorders is so strong that practitioners working with adults who are already abusing alcohol are strongly encouraged to identify whether a life event such as abuse may be responsible.

It is even clearer that activity-based addictions such as compulsive gambling, eating, and shopping, as well as sexual addictions, are not primarily caused by genetics but by the family environment and other childhood experiences. Childhood abuse and neglect in particular are key factors in developing food addictions and sexual addictions.

You may already know that your partner was emotionally, physically, or sexually abused as a child. If this is the case, open your mind and heart to the very strong possibility that this is the main reason for his substance or activity dependence. The pain of childhood abuse or neglect, especially if the abuse or neglect is ongoing, can be so unbearable that the child must find an escape from it or a way to soothe his pain. This escape or "self-medication" can come in the form of dissociation or fantasy, ingesting substances such as sugar (many addicts report that sugar was their first "drug"), or overeating. Children who are emotionally deprived or sexually abused may begin to compulsively masturbate at an early age—the precursor to sexual addiction.

Could Your Partner Have Been Abused?

If you do not know that your partner was a victim of some kind of abuse as a child but strongly suspect this is the case, it is okay to ask him. Choose a time and place when he seems open to talking (and when he is not under the influence) and start a discussion about it. You can even say that you are reading a book that points to a strong correlation between child abuse and substance dependency and you wonder if he was ever abused. However, if he seems closed to talking to you about it or flat-out denies it, drop the subject—even if you are convinced that he was, in fact, abused.

If you haven't thought of this possible connection before, you can refer to Appendix I, where we present descriptions of the various forms of childhood abuse and neglect. Although you don't want to "take your partner's inventory," as they say in AA (referring to the fourth step of "making a searching and fearless moral inventory of ourselves"), reading the material in Appendix I can still help you help your partner, even if he is not ready to admit he may have been abused.

Here's how Beverly's client Juan describes the beginning of his sexual compulsion:

I was in such constant emotional and physical pain from my father's ongoing sexual abuse that I could hardly stand it. Then I found that if I had certain sexual fantasies, such as the fantasy of me having power over someone else, my pain subsided. The first time I masturbated to one of those power fantasies I got a tremendous relief. It must be like what a heroin addict feels when they first inject the drug. The pleasure was exquisite. It washed over me, taking away all my shame and pain. I was hooked as surely as if I was a heroin addict. The next time I was overwhelmed with shame and pain I couldn't help but do the thing that I knew would take it away—at least for a time.

{EXERCISE}

PUTTING YOURSELF IN YOUR PARTNER'S PLACE

1. Imagine that you are in terrible physical pain. If you discovered that there was something available to you that would relieve that pain, wouldn't you take it?

2. Now imagine that, having taken something to relieve the pain, you discover that what you took was harmful to your body. Would you still take the substance? Even if you didn't know of anything else that would relieve your pain?

3. Imagine that what you took caused you to behave in ways that hurt you or hurt your loved ones. Would you still take the substance?

Even if you answered "no" to these questions, hopefully thinking about the dilemma your partner experiences has helped you gain some compassion for him.

People who use a substance or activity to relieve their pain or shame do not start out knowing it will get out of control. They don't know ahead of time that they will continue using even if it harms themselves or someone else. They start because they are in horrible pain and are desperate for relief—any relief. When they find that relief, whatever the form, it feels so overwhelmingly good that they are compelled to use it again—and again. The memory of the relief gets stored in their brain and in their body, and like the proverbial pigeon pecking at the bell in order to get the seed long after the supply of seed stops coming, they continue taking the substance even after they have built up such a tolerance that it no longer takes away the pain the way it used to. They increase the amount, hoping to reclaim that first experience of relief, only to find they need more and more for even a diminished effect.

Can we really blame someone who is in such severe pain for using whatever substance or activity he can find to minimize that pain? Can we fault that person for seeking that relief again, no matter how much it may harm him, when the pain returns? And can we expect a person who already feels out of control, someone who already feels terrible about himself, to care how he acts as long as he finds relief from his pain?

Gaining compassion and empathy for why your partner uses doesn't mean that you do not hold him responsible for his behavior. It just means that instead of spending your time and energy blaming and criticizing your partner for his choice to continue self-medicating, or being angry at him for taking substances or participating in activities that are harmful to him and others, you can focus on finding ways to support him.

STEP 6: ADOPTING A TRAUMA-SENSITIVE APPROACH

Our relatively new awareness of the significance childhood abuse has for addiction has changed the way professionals view substance dependence and compulsive behavior and, most importantly, how they treat those who are afflicted. While twelve-step programs are still the gold standard for many, numerous professionals now believe that the original wounding caused by childhood abuse or neglect must also be healed in order to successfully treat substance and activity dependencies.

The realization that those who suffer from dependencies also likely suffered trauma has created a new respect for the kind of trauma-sensitive treatment needed to facilitate recovery. A trauma-sensitive approach to substance and activity dependence includes understanding not only that many if not most people with dependencies suffer from posttraumatic stress disorder (PTSD) or complex trauma, but also that their behavior is, as noted in step 5, actually an understandable attempt to cope with or adapt to overwhelming circumstances. This perspective encourages us to treat those who have dependency problems with more dignity, respect, and compassion—and to encourage them to treat themselves in the same way, making it a much more empowering approach.

Substance abuse professionals who are trauma informed take this understanding a step further: They have been educated or trained in the consequences of trauma, so they can understand, anticipate, and respond to the issues, expectations, and special needs of a person who has been victimized.

The primary goal of a trauma-sensitive or trauma-informed approach is to help those who suffer from substance problems gain a better understanding of the role that trauma has played in shaping their life. Specifically, this approach focuses on helping those who suffer from dependency recognize that many of the behaviors they are most critical of in themselves (and are criticized for by others) are actually coping mechanisms or attempts at self-regulation—using drugs or alcohol to cope with anxiety, for example, or to address self-soothing deficits.

The principles of a trauma-informed way of thinking include the following:

- The impact of trauma is total: It narrows the victim's life, constricts choices, undermines self-esteem, takes away control, and creates a sense of hopelessness and helplessness.

- Many behavioral "problems" that victims experience are actually adaptive responses to trauma. Symptoms—including troubling behaviors—should be seen as *adaptations* rather than *pathology*.

- Every symptom helped a victim in the past and continues in some way to help in the present.

- The focus is on what happened to the person rather than on what is wrong with the person. Past abuses are linked to current coping strategies, and current symptoms are reframed as attempts to cope with past abuses.

- Substance use and certain psychiatric symptoms may have evolved as coping strategies at a time when options were limited.

- Those who suffer from an addiction are doing the best they can at any given time to cope with the life-altering and frequently shattering effects of trauma.

Adopting these same principles and beliefs will go a long way toward revising the way you perceive and treat your partner. Here's how this new way of thinking will help both of you:

- It *transforms him* from being "bad" to being wounded, which in turn opens the door for him to develop a more empathetic and constructive attitude toward himself.

- It *externalizes the problem*. You can now view your addicted partner as basically good, with some problems that have intruded on his life but do not represent his core being. In other words, the symptoms are the problem, not the person.

- It *normalizes the situation*. Both you and your partner may have felt that he is not normal, that he is bad, broken, sick. Trauma-informed thinking helps both of you see him as having normal and understandable reactions to unfortunate events.

- It *emphasizes strengths and resources*. Because both you and your partner are likely to be critical of him, especially of the problematic ways he has sometimes behaved, it is important to look for his strengths and give him credit for them.

- It *mobilizes him* (with your help) to discover healthier and more productive coping strategies.

Following the six steps we've outlined here will challenge your existing ideas about addiction and about those who are substance or activity dependent. These new ways of thinking and behaving will allow you to become your partner's most positive and supportive ally.

In the next chapter we will approach codependency in the same way. And if you suffer from codependency, we will explore how you can begin to heal whatever issues you may have that prevent you from being as supportive as you can be.

CHAPTER 5

A Different Perspective on Codependency

"When one is pretending, the entire body revolts."
—ANAÏS NIN

"Shame is a sickness of the soul."
—SILVAN TOMKINS

YOU MAY HAVE HEARD THAT THE ONLY TYPE OF PERSON WHO would stay with an addict is someone who is codependent. This is simply not true in every case—there isn't one type of partner any more than there is one type of substance-dependent person.

However, many partners of those who suffer from substance dependencies *are* what is normally referred to as codependent. In this chapter we are going to do for codependency what we've just done for addiction: look at it from a different perspective.

NORMALIZING CODEPENDENCY

In some respects, everyone can be codependent at times—especially if they have a partner who is substance or activity dependent. It is extremely difficult to not step in and try to "fix" a partner who has an obvious problem—to stand by and watch someone you love self-destruct. And it is especially difficult to learn when to try to help and when to let go and allow them to save themselves.

One way to start shifting our perspective is to stop labeling those who exhibit certain types of behavior as "codependent." So, from this point forward in the book, we will refer to such people as those who "practice codependent behavior," "act in codependent ways," or, regarding those who haven't established a set pattern of codependent behavior, "have codependent tendencies."

Societal norms lead many women to acquire what some would consider attributes of codependent behavior: caretaking and people-pleasing, not voicing their opinion for fear of being ridiculed or rejected, avoiding confrontation, and not expressing their own feelings for fear of hurting another person's.

Beverly describes some of these behaviors in her book *The Nice Girl Syndrome*. A "nice girl" is more concerned about what others think of her than she is about what she thinks of herself, more concerned about other people's feelings than she is about her own, and more concerned about giving people the benefit of the doubt than she is about trusting her own perceptions.

In the book Beverly outlines the four major reasons why women tend to become "nice girls": biological, cultural, familial, and experiential.

Two of these influences are common to all women. Women are hardwired biologically to (generally) be more patient and compassionate and to value connection over confrontation. In her landmark studies, Harvard University professor Carol Gilligan came to the conclusion that "female passivity" is often instead the woman's need to seek a solution that is most inclusive of everyone's needs—"an act of care rather than the restraint of aggression."

Our cultural beliefs reinforce and build on this. Girls are typically socialized to be polite, appropriate, pleasant, and agreeable—all the personality traits that characterize "nice girls." In order to attain this culturally prescribed ideal, a teenage girl must put away a great many parts of herself. She stops speaking out and expressing her feelings. Instead, she focuses on trying to please others, especially those of the opposite sex.

The other two reasons are more individual. Familial beliefs—passed on to a child either directly or by witnessing parents' and other family members' behavior—include everything from the way people should treat one another to the role women play in a family. These messages and beliefs have a powerful influence on a girl's thinking and behavior and can help shape who she becomes. Several common types of family situations can set a woman up to be a "nice girl": having a passive mother, having an abusive or tyrannical father or older brother, or being raised in a strongly misogynistic family.

In addition, it is quite common for "nice girls" to have experienced physical, emotional, or sexual abuse in their childhood or as adults. Abuse and neglect tend to create certain unhealthy attitudes and beliefs that set women up to be "nice girls" and, often, victims. Here are a few examples:

- Blaming themselves when something goes wrong

- Doubting themselves, including their perceptions, knowledge, and beliefs

- Being overly naïve and trusting of others, even when someone has proven to be untrustworthy

- Believing that their needs are not as important as those of others, and that they should meet the needs of others (especially those of their partner and children) no matter what the consequences or hardships to themselves

A NEW DEFINITION OF CODEPENDENCY:
A NEED TO CREATE A FALSE SELF

Although we want to try to stay away from labels, we do have a need for some definitions. The term *codependency* has been around for a long time, and it means different things to different people.

One commonly used definition goes something like this: *Codependency is a tendency to behave in overly passive or excessively caretaking ways that negatively impact one's relationships and quality of life. It also often involves being excessively preoccupied with the needs of others while putting one's own needs at a lower priority.*

{EXERCISE}
A CODEPENDENCY CHECKLIST

If you are concerned that you may practice codependent thinking or behavior, especially in relating to your partner, consider the following checklist:

1. I place the needs of my partner before my own and sometimes to the exclusion of my own.
2. A great deal of my attenton is focused on pleasing my partner.
3. I am often more aware of how my partner is feeling than I am of how I am feeling.
4. My fear of rejection determines what I say and/or do.
5. My fear of my partner's anger determines what I say and/or do.
6. I use giving and caretaking as a way of feeling safe in my relationship.
7. A great deal of my attention is focused on protecting my partner (making excuses for his behavior, canceling his appointments for him, and so on.).
8. A great deal of my attention is focused on solving my partner's problems or relieving my partner's pain.

9. A great deal of my attenton is focused on trying to "rescue" or change my partner.

10. A great deal of my attenton is focused on manipulating my partner into "doing things my way" (I know what he should do to solve his problems).

11. My good feelings about myself primarily stem from being liked, loved, or approved of by my partner.

12. My self-esteem is bolstered by taking care of my partner's needs and relieving his pain.

13. I withhold thoughts, opinions, or feelings because of my fear of my partner's reaction.

14. I have put my own interests and hobbies aside in order to spend time with my partner.

15. My social circle has diminished as I have involved myself with my partner and his problems.

16. I put my values aside in order to connect with my partner.

17. I value my partner's opinion and ways of doing things more than my own.

18. I spend a great deal of time worrying about and obessing over my partner's behavior.

Codependency exists on a continuum. Simple caretaking behaviors are on one end of the continuum, while far more destructive behaviors such as manipulation and controlling and abusive behaviors are on the other.

Everyone behaves in codependent ways from time to time, but some struggle with it more often and in more extreme ways. Where do you think you fit on the continuum, especially in relationship to your partner?

We believe that codependency is even more than a tendency to put one's own needs aside in order to focus on the needs and problems of others: *Codependency is a need to create a false self.*

On one end of our codependency continuum, then, we have women who use "nice girl" behaviors because of a fear of being rejected, not fitting in, hurting someone else's feelings, and so on. A woman on this end of the continuum pretends she is someone she is not in order to be accepted, pretends she wants to do things so she will be included, pretends to be a caretaker so she will be loved. She pretends she feels certain things so she won't be rejected. She pretends to care so she can be in control. (Beverly wrote extensively about this tendency to pretend in her book *Loving Him without Losing You.*)

On the other end of our continuum we have people who suffer from so much shame that they dare not show their real selves. A person on this end of the continuum may have felt such a powerful need to hide her true self that she may no longer know who her real self is, or what her true feelings are. Afraid of being shamed further—of being exposed, judged, criticized, and ultimately rejected and abandoned—she can't function as her real innate self but instead creates a false self that is centered around another person or persons.

Because shame—that overwhelming feeling of being exposed in a negative way, that feeling of humiliation that causes us to want to dig a hole and hide in it—is one of the most damaging and debilitating emotions one can experience, it is no wonder that we will go to such extreme lengths to do so. And such acute shame can cause the same profound feelings of deficiency, inferiority, unworthiness, and even self-loathing in both those who are substance dependent and those who have codependent tendencies. While those who are substance dependent use alcohol, drugs, or activities such as sex, gambling, or overeating to bury feelings of shame or to just feel "normal" in the presence of shame, codependents use their attachment and dependency on others to achieve the same goals.

It has often been noted that a woman who acts in codependent ways may be just as "addicted" to her partner as he is to his drug or activity of choice. In fact, some have called codependency a "love addiction." Those who are addicted to love, relationships, and romance look to others to provide not only companionship, but distraction from their own lives, validation of their worthiness or lovableness, and even a reason to live.

> *Chris: In* Recover to Live, *my book about the seven toxic compulsions behind addiction, I classify codependency as the unofficial eighth toxic compulsion. Codependency and addiction have a lot in common, and I discovered in recovery that I had codependent tendencies as well. Getting a handle on my codependency has taken twice as long as it did for me to get clean and sober. For most people I know, that is the norm. If you have spent a lifetime believing that there is an answer to your human discomfort that exists outside yourself—in a pill, glass, or activity—it's not hard to transfer that belief onto another person. Like codependents, those suffering from active addiction often utilize relationships, marriage, and parenthood as ways to avoid their primary issue—which is always themselves.*

The bottom line? True codependency is a way to create a false self in order to avoid further shaming experiences and to compensate for feelings of shame. This false self is the persona or mask that the world sees. And those who create this false self become increasingly out of touch with their real self. This can lead to two secondary, but equally powerful problems: *feelings of emptiness* and *lack of self-awareness*.

Feelings of Emptiness

Emptiness is usually felt as a vague experience of restlessness, boredom, or numbness. It can take the form of a feeling of being disconnected, as if you are just going through the motions or sleepwalking through life; a feeling of not belonging; or a feeling that your life is not important or lacks meaning.

If you have been out of touch with or denied your feelings for a long time, you may be overwhelmed with feelings of boredom or apathy when you are alone. Some people combat emptiness through success, power, accomplishments, or attention, thereby developing an insatiable need for validation, recognition, or understanding, and so when those needs are not being met, they feel anxious and empty.

Feelings of emptiness often underlie the fear of abandonment. And feelings of emptiness are intensified when we feel lonely or disassociated. Remember the findings of the Rat Park experiments: Humans have a powerful need for connection with others, and if we do not get that need fulfilled, we will look for anything to bond with, drugs or alcohol included. The same is true for those who behave in codependent ways. Because of feelings of disconnection—from the self and others—those with codependent tendencies attach themselves to another person in order to avoid feelings of emptiness.

Many people with codependent tendencies attempt to fill their emptiness by living through or controlling other people. Others are drawn to drama and conflict, often in the form of unavailable partners, substance-dependent partners, and abusers. While they claim to consider stable, healthy people boring, the truth is that they need all that drama and conflict to keep them from having to face their emptiness.

Lack of Self-Awareness

Those who suffer from codependent tendencies focus all their energy outside themselves—mostly on other people—because they are afraid of what they will find if they look inside themselves.

Perhaps not surprisingly, this creates a lack of self-awareness. If you're doing everything you can to avoid what's going on inside you, how can you know what you are feeling? And if you don't know what you are feeling at any given time, how do you really know who you are, what you desire, or how to take care of yourself?

EMOTIONAL ISSUES RELATED TO CODEPENDENT BEHAVIOR

Using our definition of codependency—a need to create a false self in order to be accepted and loved and to avoid further shaming—we can see that codependent behavior is also a way for people to avoid dealing with certain issues, issues that often originate in childhood. Let's examine these one by one.

Overwhelming Feelings of Shame

As we've already seen, shame underscores many of the general emotional issues that those with codependent tendencies suffer from. When we feel shamed—when we feel, deep inside, exposed and unworthy—we want to hide. It shows in our bodies: We hang our heads, stoop our shoulders, and curve inward as if trying to become invisible. These physical manifestations are often accompanied by thoughts like "I'm a total failure" or "I'm so stupid." People who have been deeply shamed take on the underlying, pervasive belief that they are defective, unacceptable, or unlovable.

Shame can also cause us to feel isolated. In many cultures historically, when people broke a society's rules, they were banished. Being shamed feels like being banished—unworthy to be around others.

In addition to feeling separated from others, shame can cause us to feel separated from our real self. As a self-protective measure, we may create elaborate masks—smiling, pleasing others, trying to appear self-confident—in order to cover up our real self and have others see us as better than we feel we are.

Low Self-Esteem

Low self-esteem, a frequent result of chronic shame, is at the center of nearly all symptoms of codependent behavior. It affects our willingness to take care of ourselves, especially in relationships. It affects our ability to communicate our needs, feelings, and thoughts in clear, assertive ways, and it affects how we allow others to talk to us. It also affects our ability to set appropriate boundaries and even our belief that we have a right to set them.

If you have low self-esteem and perceive yourself as "less than" or unworthy of love and respect, you are likely to attract a partner who sees you in the same way. You may also be drawn to someone who is unavailable (for example, a man who is so dependent on a substance or activity that he has no time or energy for a real relationship). You will feel as if you don't deserve to be loved and so will push away people who show you love. Or you might acknowledge that other people love you but not believe you are loved for your real self ("If he only knew the real me . . .").

Abandonment Issues

Many of those with codependent tendencies suffer from a fear of abandonment, usually brought on by actual abandonment—physical or emotional—as a child.

Physical or emotional abandonment can cause a child (and later, an adult) to feel afraid, lost, insecure, and overwhelmed when they have to be away from a loved one, even for a short time. While those without abandonment issues can be away from their partner for even extended periods of time without having an emotional meltdown, those who were abandoned suffer from so much fear and anxiety that they try to avoid separation as much as possible. One of the best ways to guarantee that you don't have to experience separation is to *become indispensable to your partner;* that way, you think, he won't want to be away from you.

Fear of Intimacy

It may seem like a contradiction to say that those with codependent tendencies have a fear of intimacy, since many are dependent and fearful of rejection or abandonment. But fear of intimacy is just the flip side of fear of abandonment: If you never become truly intimate with someone, you don't have to risk having them reject or abandon you.

A fear of intimacy can manifest in surprising ways, such as continually choosing to be involved with those who are unavailable (married, unwilling to be faithful, unable to commit) or those who cannot become emotionally intimate or sustain such intimacy—including those who have substance or activity dependencies.

Dependency Issues

Many of those who suffer from codependent tendencies remain dependent on others for motivation, validation, and guidance on how they should live their lives. Although they may appear to be confident and successful on the outside, they are dependent on others' approval to feel worthy and lovable.

Children who are not encouraged to become independent can become afraid to take risks, insecure about their ability to take care of themselves, and unable to trust their own instincts.

Control Issues

Those with codependent tendencies attempt to control other people, their environment, and their emotions. Their lives may feel so out of control that *the only way they can gain a sense of control is to attempt to control others.*

Shame can be a factor here as well. Those with codependent tendencies often try to control other people's behaviors and feelings in order to feel better about themselves and to avoid their own shame.

In fact, the greater their shame and emptiness, the greater their anxiety and thus the greater that need to control. They may try to be perfect, lest they be criticized by others and be further shamed. And because they perceive their partners as extensions of themselves, they require them to be perfect as well.

Those who are codependent are also motivated to control others because their very dependence leaves them feeling vulnerable. As a way of countering these vulnerable feelings, they may use control tactics that can become emotionally abusive, such as anger, blame, isolation, unreasonable demands, the silent treatment, and withholding attention, affection, money, or sex.

Caretaking Behaviors

For those who have codependent tendencies, caretaking is actually a form of passive control and can be quite manipulative. Codependent caretaking, in contrast to genuine caregiving, stems from shame. It is an attempt by the codependent person to raise her self-esteem and increase her pride in herself by focusing on her partner and his flaws, thus allowing her to hide her needs, her feelings, and her own flaws, which she is too ashamed to reveal.

Codependent caretaking is giving in order to get love. In other words, there are strings attached to your giving: "I'll give to you or I'll help you so you'll love and accept me." You attend to others' emotional needs by listening, advising, solving their problems, and accommodating their requests. You please others, take care of others, and self-sacrifice in order to ensure that you are needed and loved and, perhaps most important, that you won't be abandoned.

You may go to great lengths to be needed—by your partner and your children, at your job, even with your friends. You make yourself indispensable. You give more than is required because you don't feel needed, valued, or lovable unless you do.

Some go to the extreme of making helping others an obsession, such as offering advice or help when it is unsolicited and even not wanted. In return they want acknowledgment, gratitude, and love, and if they don't receive it, they feel unappreciated, resentful, and angry.

In a relationship with a partner who has a substance or activity dependence, caretaking and control issues can escalate. The more you do for your partner—the more you rescue him from the negative consequences of his substance use by doing things like making excuses for his being late or hiding his drinking from family members—the more his irresponsible and self-destructive behaviors drive your need for control. You become increasingly frustrated, angry, and desperate. Even those who are truly motivated by love can begin to blame and judge and try to change their partner in order to avoid their own deeper feelings of pain and inadequacy. But all your efforts to change your partner by nagging and blaming only heap more shame on him and provide him with a welcome justification to blame and abuse you and to continue using.

FACING THE TRUTH

Do you identify with any of the issues we've just discussed? Answering this question is, of course, easier said than done, since if you do suffer from codependent behaviors, you may feel disconnected from yourself and your true feelings. But if you do identify with these issues, and you can break through your fears and resistance to face them, you will be taking a giant step in the direction of your own healing—as well as the healing of your relationship.

While you may not wish to label yourself a "codependent," if you have certain codependent behaviors or tendencies, they need to be addressed if you wish to be as helpful as possible to your partner, as well as be an emotionally healthy person. Of course, some code-pendent behaviors are much more detrimental to both you and your substance-dependent partner than others. A need to be in control can cause you to become bossy or demanding, insisting that he get help or that he get home at a certain hour, threatening to leave if he doesn't "shape up." As we have discussed, and you have no doubt discovered, these tactics do not work—in fact, they more often backfire, making your partner rebellious.

Just as those who are substance dependent look to a substance or activity to provide relief, self-soothing, and stress reduction, you may look to your partner and your relationship for the same reasons. This might be a fair assessment for many of you reading this book. It is much easier to focus on your partner's problems than to look at your own. In fact, your partner's issues may just be a distraction that helps you avoid yourself and your own issues.

These words are not meant to be a criticism. Rather, they are an attempt to help you understand yourself better and hopefully be a catalyst for a major shift in your thinking. The point is this: It is likely that you need as much help as your partner. And just as we encourage you to have compassion for your partner's dependency and the suffering that drives it, you deserve compassion for yours, too.

WHAT CAUSES CODEPENDENT BEHAVIOR?

The first and perhaps most important step in changing your codependent behavior is to work on having compassion for yourself. One of the ways of doing this is to gain more understanding for why you are the way you are. Self-compassion naturally follows self-understanding.

When you uncover and heal the source of the shame that underlies your codependent behavior and thinking, you free your real self to emerge. This means you can (1) stop pretending, (2) stop taking care of others as a way to prove your worthiness, (3) stop trying to be perfect to avoid further shaming, and (4) stop trying to make yourself indispensable in order to avoid being rejected or abandoned.

Our false (codependent) self is usually rooted in childhood and due to one of the following circumstances:

1. *Having codependent parents.* Codependent parents tend to have weak interpersonal boundaries—that is, they see their child as an extension of themselves—or are unable to empathize and instead use their child to meet their own needs, build up their self-esteem, and fulfill their ideals.

    Healthy parents understand that they need to support their child's sense of separateness. This means that they gradually begin to let go of control and trust that their child will do the right thing and take care of themselves. They also encourage and accept their child's uniqueness by respecting their individual thoughts, feelings, and needs rather than trying to make them into replicas of themselves.

    Unfortunately, some parents are limited by their own unmet emotional needs and lack of individuation. Some look to their children for the validation, self-esteem, comfort, or companionship they did not receive from their own parents. Others resist their child's efforts to set boundaries or spread their wings by being overly protective or overly possessive. Some parents have their own abandonment issues, and when these are triggered they have difficulty letting go, undermining their child's independence by telling them things like "You're going to get hurt" or "You only think of yourself."

2. *Lack of parental validation.* Because your parents did not validate your real self, including your feelings, needs, and perceptions, you may have begun to believe that your feelings and needs were wrong or unimportant. To

obtain connection and approval from your parents, you may have suppressed your true feelings, needs, and wants, which may in turn have impaired the healthy growth of an autonomous self. "As your real self started to disappear, codependency was born, impeding your natural individuation—the process of owning and trusting perceptions, thoughts, feelings, and memories and becoming a separate individual cognitively, emotionally, and psychologically."[22]

A persistent failure on a parent's part to empathize with and validate a child's real self can also generate shame in a child. When a child doesn't feel understood or doesn't observe validation in her parent's facial expression, voice, and touch, she feels unlovable and alone. And because her parents have not acknowledged and validated her feelings or have criticized them, she will tend to question her own thoughts and feelings, thus becoming more and more disconnected from herself.

3. *Emotional or physical abandonment.* When emotional and/or physical abandonment recurs on a regular basis, a child can become overwhelmed with shame and lose the connection with her real self.

While emotional neglect—receiving little or no affection or physical nurturing, not being listened to or focused on—is a clear case of emotional abandonment, a parent's lack of emotional connection to his or her child can also be felt as abandonment. Some mothers, for example, are unable to emotionally bond with their infants, often because their own mother was unable to bond with them. In other situations, children may be aware that their parents did not plan to have them and still do not want them. Children tend to blame themselves for their parents' lack of concern or caring, assuming that there is something about them that is unacceptable or unlovable—that they are simply bad, inadequate, unimportant, or unworthy of a loving relationship.

Physical abandonment by a parent, whether it is complete abandonment in the case of a parent permanently leaving a child in the care of someone else or frequently leaving a child alone while they are at work or at the bar, can cause a child to fear being alone and fear rejection as an adult, thus causing her to cling to even the most abusive or substance-dependent partner.

4.   *Other neglect or abuse in childhood.* There is a strong correlation between codependent behavior and childhood trauma such as child abuse and neglect. For this reason it is important for you to look closely at the possibility that you were neglected or abused—if you are not already aware of it.

   If you were physically or sexually abused as a child, you are probably aware of it and you probably suffer from the effects of that abuse every day. But there are other, less obvious forms of abuse that you may not be aware of, and they can be just as damaging as physical and sexual abuse. Please refer to Appendix I for more information on exactly what constitutes child abuse.

UNDERSTANDING THE CONNECTION BETWEEN CODEPENDENT BEHAVIORS AND CHILDHOOD ABUSE AND NEGLECT

If you were abused or neglected in childhood, it is highly possible that this abuse has at least contributed to if not caused your codependent behavior or ways of thinking. You've likely noticed a strong similarity between the types of issues and behaviors we've described concerning codependency and the items outlined in the following sections.

See if you recognize the following behaviors in yourself and then try to connect these behaviors with your experiences of neglect or abuse.

Hypervigilance

Abused children tend to become *hypervigilant*, meaning that they are so afraid of being yelled at, criticized, hit, or otherwise abused that they are on constant alert for signs that their abusive parent is getting upset. This state of hyperarousal can stay with an abused child well into adulthood, causing her to carefully watch her partner for any signs of disapproval, indications that he might be getting upset, or signals that he might be preparing to engage in substance abuse or compulsive behavior.

> *"I watch my partner too closely, making him feel like he is 'under a microscope.' I realize now that I do this because as a child I got in the habit of watching my father closely to see if he was getting angry. When I saw signs of anger on his face I made sure I got as far away from him as I could get."*

External Focus

Being hypervigilant in turn causes a child to become *externally focused* as a method of self-protection. An externally focused person is so intent on the moods, needs, and feelings of her partner that she ignores (or may not even be aware of) her own.

Children who are abused are taught that their abuser's feelings, needs, and desires supersede their own. This is especially true for children who are sexually abused.

"I constantly focus on my partner's behavior instead of my own. I scrutinize his behavior to see if he is doing anything wrong. I now realize that in a weird way I do this so I don't get into trouble, since I see him as an extension of myself."

Pleasing and Placating Behavior

Along with being hypervigilant and developing an external focus, abused and neglected children learn to do whatever it takes to please their parents, either in order to avoid their anger or punishment or as a way of getting much-needed attention. Children who adopt this behavior, commonly referred to as *people pleasing*, tend to carry it forward into adulthood.

"I constantly try to please my husband (and others) and then I become angry when he doesn't return the favor. I build up resentment and take on a 'poor me' attitude. I realize now that the only way I could get any attention or love from my mother was to be the 'good little girl' and go out of my way to do things for her that I knew she liked, such as cleaning the house and taking care of my siblings. I also realize that I'm angry at my mother for not loving me for who I am, and a lot of that anger comes out at my husband."

Low Self-Worth

When a child is emotionally and/or physically neglected—when her parents ignore her when she talks and fail to provide her with physical affection or to satisfy her need for comfort or adequate food, shelter, or clothing—a child comes to the conclusion that she is unlovable. After all, she reasons, if her own parents don't love her, there must be something wrong with her.

Because she feels so bad about herself, it is highly likely that an abused or neglected child will attract and be attracted to men who do not respect her or even to men who treat her the way her parents treated her, either abusing her or neglecting her. She feels so bad about herself that she doesn't believe she deserves to be treated with respect, kindness, and consideration.

If one or both of a child's parents were addicted to a substance (alcohol, drugs) or an activity (work, gambling), and this contributed to them being either neglectful or abusive, the child may grow up to marry a replica of this parent.

> *"I now realize that I married my husband because I didn't believe I deserved any better. I knew he had a drinking problem when I married him, but he was the only man who had proposed to me. My mother always told me that no man could ever love me, and I guess I believed her."*

Failure or Disappointment in Self

As we have seen, child abuse and neglect cause children to feel horrific shame, which can negatively affect their self-esteem, their belief in themselves, their ability to learn, and their belief that they deserve good things. These self-beliefs can profoundly affect motivation and success in school and in professional endeavors. Even if an abused child experiences success, it is likely that her low self-worth will cause her to still feel disappointed in herself and her achievements. This can lead her to focus instead on her partner's abilities and success. Abused children may be drawn to powerful, successful partners as a way of compensating for what they perceive as their failures or even as a way of vicariously living through them.

> *"I married my husband because he owned a successful business and everyone around him looked up to him. I thought marrying him would help me feel better about myself since my parents mistreated me and abandoned me and made me feel like I was worthless. Unfortunately, I failed to see that he was controlling*

and neglectful, just like my parents. Even when I came to my senses and realized what I had done, I felt so bad about myself that I put up with his behavior but resented him for it, just like I resented my parents."

Shame Anxiety

Shame anxiety is the anticipation of experiencing shame and abandonment. The fear of further shaming can make former abuse victims act overly solicitous and helpful and become hypersensitive to any sign of disapproval or abandonment from others. They tend to fret about what they will say or do, or see hidden meanings in other people's reactions.

Perfectionism

Some people who were abused in childhood grow up to be perfectionists. Their focus on doing everything absolutely perfectly is an attempt to guarantee their safety; if they never make a mistake, they believe, they will not give others a reason to punish or shame them again.

A Need to Be in Control

Some carry this need for perfection to an extreme and become controlling of others. For example, if they took on the role of protector of younger siblings, they may have tried to protect them by controlling their siblings' behavior (inspecting their faces and teeth to make sure they were clean in order to avoid them being yelled at by their mother, making sure they did their chores in order to prevent them from being hit by their father).

Another reason former abuse victims may become controlling, especially in personal relationships, is that they felt out of control during their childhood—for example, if they came from a chaotic household where their parents often fought with one another or where one or both of their parents drank alcohol to excess or abused drugs.

> *"My mother was always criticizing me. I could never please her no matter how hard I tried. And so I became a perfectionist. I did everything perfectly so she couldn't find fault in me. I realize now that I transferred my own need to be perfect to a need for my partner to be perfect, too, and this caused me to become controlling, critical, and even emotionally abusive at times—just like my mother."*

Caretaking and "Fixer" Behavior

Abuse victims who had a parent or parents with a substance problem may have taken on the role of the "fixer" in their home: putting a drunk parent to bed, taking care of siblings because a parent was passed out, making excuses for a parent's behavior when people asked about him. As an adult they may unconsciously seek out the same "fixer" role by marrying or becoming involved with someone with a substance problem.

> *"My parents were both alcoholics, and I essentially grew up parenting my two siblings, keeping the house clean, and cooking all the meals. I got a sense of accomplishment for playing that role, so I continued it into adulthood. I ended up doing my friends' homework in high school and I was always the one to drive when my friends were too drunk. People always came to me with their problems. When I met my husband I realize now that I just continued this pattern. He always had problems and I was always the one to solve them. Now I'm trying to do it with his drug problem."*

{**EXERCISE**}

CONNECTING THE DOTS

1. Think about how the behavior you took on as a way of coping with childhood neglect or abuse could have turned into some of the codependent behaviors you now exhibit.
2. Make a list of these behaviors and "connect the dots" between your childhood experiences and your current codependent behaviors.

FOCUS ON YOUR OWN ISSUES

As you've learned, codependent behavior and codependent thinking are really about you, not your partner. Codependency is a way of avoiding your own problems—of taking your focus off yourself and putting it on him.

It is much easier to recognize what is wrong with someone else, and it is much easier to come up with ideas about how the other person can solve their problems, than it is to recognize and address our own issues. If we do manage to actually focus on ourselves long enough to see our faults and shortcomings, we often make excuses for ourselves and rationalize our actions (or inaction). We compare ourselves with others and convince ourselves that since others have the same problems, ours are not so bad. Sometimes we even convince ourselves that we are *better* than other people.

The truth is, you may be lying to yourself. You may be pretending you are okay when underneath your avoidance, your excuses, and perhaps your bravado, you know you have issues you need to work on. If you were willing and able to focus on yourself, you probably wouldn't have time to put so much focus on your partner's problems. You wouldn't have as much time to count how many drinks he has, or how much food he is eating, or whether or not he is watching porn. You would offer your partner help when and if he needed it, but then you would go back to solving your own problems.

{EXERCISE}

YOUR ISSUES—A SELF-ASSESSMENT

If you think you may exhibit codependent behaviors or thinking, a good way to begin focusing on and working through your own issues is to ask yourself the following questions:

1. What issues might I be avoiding by focusing so much attention on my partner's problems?
2. Are there wounds from my childhood that I have never addressed? Examples: childhood neglect, abandonment, abuse
3. Are there issues from my childhood that I started to address but put aside when I got involved with my partner or when his problems became evident?
4. In addition to my codependent behavior and thinking, do I have a dependency problem that I do not currently address sufficiently, or at all? Examples: a dependency on sugar, coffee, cigarettes, shopping, hoarding
5. What might be the underlying reasons that I became involved with my partner? Examples: my father was an alcoholic and I'm trying to rescue my husband because I couldn't rescue him, my mother was verbally abusive in the same way my husband gets when he's using drugs, I was sexually abused as a child and my partner has a sex addiction

As you continue with this book and with your attempts to help your partner, be on the lookout for codependent behaviors and ways of thinking in yourself. Remember that while you are supporting your partner in his recovery, it is also important that you focus on your own.

In the next chapter you will begin to learn how to shift your codependent behaviors to compassionate ones. As you learn to practice these compassionate behaviors toward your partner, remember to apply them to yourself as well.

PART III.

YOUR ROLE IN YOUR PARTNER'S RECOVERY

CHAPTER 6

The Difference between Codependency and Compassion

"Compassion is the radicalism of our time."
—THE DALAI LAMA

NOW THAT WE'VE CHANGED THE WAY YOU LOOK AT ADDIC-
tion and codependency, it's time to talk about what you can do to
help your partner move toward recovery.

Although you have the power to help your partner, it is important
to understand that there are certain attitudes and behaviors, especially those associated with codependency, that will not be helpful
and may even hinder your partner's progress. These ways of interact-
ing may cause him to push back or, worse, pretend to comply while
holding more tightly to the status quo. There are also certain attitudes and behaviors, those rooted in compassion, that you will need
to take on in order to maximize the amount of help and support you
can provide.

This chapter discusses these attitudes and behaviors, as well as
the sometimes subtle differences between supporting your partner in
seeking recovery and getting in his way, taking over, or what is commonly referred to as "enabling" him.

THE DIFFERENCE BETWEEN CODEPENDENT BEHAVIOR AND COMPASSIONATE BEHAVIOR

When it comes to helping a partner with substance abuse problems, the line between codependency and compassion can be fuzzy because the intentions of both appear to be the same. But while compassion promotes effective communication and mutual respect, codependency can destroy the foundation of even the healthiest relationship.

When we are being truly compassionate, our intentions are motivated by *love and selflessness*. In contrast, the underlying motive of codependency is *self-protection*. As we discussed in the previous chapter, the person exhibiting codependent behaviors and thinking needs to be needed; she pursues acceptance and safety in an effort to avoid abandonment. In this way, codependent actions—although seemingly charitable—are often closer to selfish than selfless.

As we saw in chapter 3, thinking and behaving compassionately can make us feel good in a variety of ways, activating pleasure circuits in the brain and the secretion of the "bonding" hormone oxytocin. It slows down our heart rate, makes us more resilient to stress, and boosts our immune system. In contrast, codependent thinking and actions deplete our energy and leave us wanting; they can generate a "hangover" feeling similar to the one many addictions produce and can take a toll on our emotional and physical health.

While both compassionate and codependent behavior may involve attending to the needs of others, and can at times involve personal sacrifice, a compassionate person continues to care for herself in the process; she never abandons herself or her own needs in order to take care of another. The person acting in codependent ways, on the other hand, discards her own needs, replacing them with the needs of the other person. And when she finds herself emotionally and physically exhausted at the end of the day, she often becomes bitter, resentful, and frustrated.

Compassion strengthens the foundation of a relationship. Acts of selflessness contribute to mutual appreciation, effective communication, trust, and other key ingredients of successful relationships. In contrast, codependency deteriorates relationships, causing dependency, jealousy, bitterness, destructive behavior, poor communication, and a host of other problems.

When you are showing compassion and care toward someone, both people come away from the situation feeling energized, empowered, and encouraged, not frustrated, angry, or depleted.

Compassionate Giving versus Codependent Giving

Those who suffer from codependent ways of thinking can feel as though they don't have a choice when it comes to taking care of their partner. They tend to have an exaggerated sense of responsibility, as well as a fear of abandonment if they don't do what their partner wants or needs. They can also feel imprisoned by a sense that something terrible will happen to their partner if they don't attend to his needs. A compassionate person, on the other hand, is aware that she has a choice and makes her decision to help at any given time carefully and thoughtfully.

These are the keys to giving in a compassionate way:

- You do so in a deeply *selfless* way as opposed to a *self-based* way.

- You aren't hooked on the results. You offer information, resources, prayers, and other forms of help, but then you let go and allow your partner to make his own choices.

- You offer a listening ear without trying to fix his problems for him.

- You seek to support your partner in his own journey while refraining from creating an unhealthy dependence on you.

- You balance kindness with the willingness to say no when saying yes would hurt either of you.

The Motives Check

Another way to determine whether you are acting from a place of compassion versus a place of codependency is to do a motives check. Ask yourself these questions:

- Is helping my partner a way for me to distract myself from my own issues?
- Do I want to "rescue" my partner because it makes me feel worthwhile, good, needed, important, or proud?
- Am I helping my partner because my identity depends on my ability to help others?

If you are completely honest with yourself, you may discover that you answered yes to some or all of these questions. If this is the case, it is highly likely that codependency, not compassion, is driving your behavior.

ENABLING BEHAVIORS

Contrary to popular belief, research has shown that not all partners who stay with substance and activity abusers are what those in the recovery movement call "enablers"—but, unfortunately, many are.

Enabling behavior includes anything that is intended to "fix" a problem created by your partner's substance dependence—everything from calling his boss to say he is sick when he is actually hungover, to making excuses to friends and family for his inappropriate behavior ("he's under a lot of stress"), to buying alcohol in the hope that he'll drink at home rather than go out and risk a car accident.

While your intention may be to help your partner, the result is the opposite: Showing him that you will always be there to fix what goes wrong sends the message that you accept his inappropriate behavior. You may scold, nag, or lecture with your words, but your behavior says, "Don't worry, I'll always be here to make it easier for you."

Being so "helpful" also accomplishes two other very *un*helpful things:

1. You drain yourself to the point that you are running on empty, leaving little energy to do the positive things you could be doing to help your partner.

2. You make it easier for your partner to continue his substance abuse—as long as you are there to fix things, rescue him, clean up the mess, or smooth things over, your partner does not have to face the consequences that might otherwise drive him to make a change.

Chris: Often when an addicted person is in the throes of active addiction, we use relationships to give us what we think we need. A place to crash, or someone to buy our drugs, give us sex, make us feel alive—you name it, and an addict has found someone to give it to him. We are really good at getting others to give us what we want. The problem is that what we think we need is usually the last thing you should give us. When we get what we think we need from you, it doesn't work for very long. So, what does the addicted person do next? Do we think that maybe what we are after is the wrong thing for us? No way—we get rid of the person who gave it to us, or we turn to our substance or activity of choice even further to cope. We do the same thing over and over again, thinking we will get a different result—the very definition of insanity. It's a vicious cycle that doesn't end until someone leaves, dies, or gets well in recovery.

Let's look at some enabling behaviors that need to be avoided because they impede your partner's progress.

Fixing

Fixing refers to behaviors that rescue your partner from the negative effects of his actions—for example, making sure he gets to work on time because he abused drugs the night before, bringing him a cool washcloth and aspirin in the morning to help nurse his hangover, or cutting back on your own spending in order to pay household bills because your partner has lost so much money gambling. Both science and experience tell us that if a substance abuser is prevented from facing the negative consequences of his actions, his behavior is not going to change; instead, things will likely get progressively worse.

Fixing behaviors may *feel* like the loving, humane, or sensible thing to do, but what they really do is prevent your partner from having to fix his mistakes himself. Picking up your partner from the bar because he is so drunk that he forgot where he parked his car seems like something that helps him; after all, you don't want him wandering around drunk. But it might be better to tell him to take a cab. Sure, the cab might cost him an arm and a leg, but having to pay for it might help him face the consequences of his actions.

The same is true when you drive all over town trying to find his car or call local towing companies to see if his car was impounded: Better to let him find his car himself the next day, once he has sobered up.

Each time you fix a situation, it reinforces your partner's belief that no matter how irresponsible or self-destructive his behavior, there are no consequences. He knows that you always take care of everything, so he doesn't have to. If you really want to motivate your partner to give up his self-destructive behaviors, you absolutely must allow him to be responsible for his own mistakes—indeed, his own life.

Protecting

There is a subtle but important distinction between *fixing* and *protecting:* Fixing behaviors tend to *solve* problems so that your partner doesn't have to face the consequences of his actions, while protecting behaviors *shield* your partner from having to face the truth about himself and his substance dependence. Protecting behaviors can also protect your partner by preventing others from seeing the truth about your partner's substance or activity dependence.

While it may seem as if protecting your partner is a loving thing to do, you are in fact preventing him from learning how to protect himself. So, ironically, to truly protect your partner you must first *stop* protecting him, so that he is motivated to protect himself—ideally, by getting help to stop the behavior that's endangering him in the first place.

{EXERCISE}

ARE YOU A PROTECTOR?

Do any of the following scenarios sound familiar?

1. I have made excuses to friends or family members for my partner's failure to show up at a planned event, or made excuses to our children when he didn't attend their baseball game, recital, or school open house.
2. I have made excuses for my partner's inappropriate behavior when he got drunk or stoned at a party or when we were having dinner with friends.
3. I have avoided making plans with friends or family because I was afraid my partner would get drunk or high on drugs and become argumentative or inappropriate in some other way, such as becoming too flirtatious.
4. I have paid off my partner's gambling debts because I was afraid he would get beaten up by the people he owes.

5. I have paid off my partner's credit card to prevent it from being taken away.

6. I have paid an overdue bar bill or covered a bad check to prevent the owner from banning my partner from the premises or taking legal action.

7. I have hidden my partner's problem from family and friends.

8. I have consoled my partner when he felt guilt, shame, or remorse.

9. I have downplayed the seriousness of my partner's problem—either to him or to others.

If you aren't sure whether you are contributing to your partner's self-destructive behaviors by fixing or protecting, try asking yourself these questions:

- *Do I make excuses to myself and others for my partner's bad behaviors and judgment?* This might include minimizing your partner's substance or activity dependence by calling it a "passing phase," or contacting his boss with excuses for why he failed to show up for work.

- *Do I remain silent in order to avoid confrontations and arguments?* Remaining silent for fear of losing your partner's love protects him from facing the truth. And avoiding confrontation for fear of being subjected to verbal or physical abuse when you voice an opinion suggests that your partner is abusive, not just someone with a dependency problem. While your intention may be to protect yourself from negative consequences, you are preventing him (and possibly yourself) from facing the truth.

- *Do I take on responsibilities that should rightfully be my partner's?* This might include paying his bills, babysitting his children on his visitation days, visiting his parents in the hospital or a convalescent home, or buying flowers for his secretary.

BEHAVIORS THAT BLOCK YOUR PARTNER'S RECOVERY

While fixing and protecting behaviors do not help your partner because they enable him to continue his self-destructive behaviors, other behaviors actually *prevent* your partner from recovering. These blocking behaviors include any action or attitude on your part that acts as a deterrent to your partner's recovery.

Shaming

Shaming, which we talked about in chapter 2, is a classic example of a blocking behavior. For one thing, shaming can cause your partner to become defensive, which may make him unwilling to cooperate in his own recovery. But in addition, it can actually cause your partner to feel worse about himself, which may lead him to lose his motivation to recover. Similar behaviors likely to cause him to become defensive and feel bad about himself include nagging, criticizing, and throwing past mistakes in his face.

Arguing

Arguing with your partner is another example of a blocking behavior. Those who are substance dependent have a tendency to blame others for their problems, especially their partners. If you argue with your partner about his using, you essentially give him an excuse to blame you for his problems. For example, he can accuse you of always having to be right, or of not understanding him, and then blame his drinking on these things. And like shaming and criticizing, arguing provokes defensiveness, which in turn undermines motivation.

If you are in the habit of arguing, notice what happens to you just before you start—the tight jaw, the crossed arms, the tension in your chest. Similarly, take note of the clues that your partner may be feeling defensive and getting ready to argue—the clenched fists, the pacing across the floor. These can all be cues that you need to take a deep breath, step back, and connect with yourself. Notice the emotions you are feeling—anger or fear or sadness—and remind yourself that you have a right to feel these things. Remind yourself that *you* are responsible for your feelings, not your partner.

Another effective strategy to help stop arguments is understanding why they start in the first place. We often argue when we are actually feeling ambivalent about the situation ourselves. When our partner presents an opposing view, we may be arguing against our own ambivalence. Taking a few minutes to connect with yourself could reveal this truth. Backing off can also give your partner a chance to connect with himself and discover what he is really feeling. And it can allow him to confront his own ambivalence, so that he starts to argue with himself instead of defending against what you are saying.

Another reason people argue is that they don't feel heard. Even though you may not agree with what your partner is saying, you can always tell him, "I hear you" or "I understand what you are saying" or "I understand how you feel." These are *validating statements*, meant to express to your partner that he has a right to his feelings and that you do, in fact, hear him and understand him, even if you don't agree with him. Being heard and being validated are two of the most important needs that we as humans have. Once your partner feels validated and heard, a great deal of his resistance, anger, and need to argue may fade.

People also become defensive and argumentative when they feel they are being forced to take one side of an issue or to defend their position. One way around this is for you to acknowledge that there can be two sides to the argument—that both of you can have valid points and valid reasons for your feelings.

Beverly's client Marlene was married to Dan, a compulsive gambler in recovery. His best friend Jim was having a bachelor party at a casino in Atlantic City, and Marlene was horrified at the possibility that her husband would experience a relapse if he went. The two of them had been arguing about the situation for weeks.

In one of her sessions, Beverly encouraged Marlene to stop arguing with her husband and to instead offer him some understanding and compassion. The next week she reported: "I told him, as compassionately as I could, that I understood that it was important for him to go to Jim's bachelor party. Then I asked him if he could understand why it scared me to think about him going to Atlantic City since the last time he was there he lost a lot of money gambling."

Since Marlene expressed understanding for Dan's point of view, while at the same time offering her own, he had less of a need to justify to her his reasons for wanting to go.

Beverly also suggested that they approach the situation as a dilemma that the two of them could work on together rather than as an argument in which each of them presented only one side. By doing so, Marlene would be inviting Dan to acknowledge his own ambivalence, which could help him see the potential consequences of attending the bachelor party more fully.

Often people pretend that they have no ambivalence, because they are too busy trying to convince us that they are doing the right thing. They may believe that the benefits of their behavior (in Dan's case, supporting his friend) outweigh the costs (relapsing). If we label their thinking "denial" or call it foolish or selfish and don't take what they have to say about the benefits seriously, we're likely to get stuck defending our side of the argument all by ourselves rather than helping the other person see the full picture.

Tone of Voice

How you communicate with your partner can have a major impact on his openness to your help and support. Indeed, the tone you take when you speak to your partner matters as much as—or in some cases more than—your actual words. If your tone is guilt-producing—if it is self-pitying or whining—your partner is likely to put up a defensive wall in order to avoid feeling shame.

An abusive tone can be just as damaging as abusive words. A sarcastic or mocking tone can be considered emotionally abusive, and the same holds true if your tone is scolding, demanding, belittling, or demeaning. Your partner is not a child (even if you feel that he acts like one at times) and doesn't need you to remind him of how "bad" he is. Examples of other emotionally abusive communication behaviors include rolling your eyes, making faces, making sounds depicting disapproval or mocking, and giving your partner the cold shoulder or the silent treatment.

The point here is not that you shouldn't express your feelings about your partner's substance use. You need to be able to do so, but in ways—and at times—that are constructive for you and for your partner. For example, it will not be constructive to try to talk to your partner when he is drunk or high. Nor is it a good idea to talk to him when he has a hangover.

To have any hope of getting through to your partner, you need to talk to him in a kind, supportive, collaborative way. If you can't manage this at a particular moment, wait to speak to him until you can, or at least try to sound neutral—as if you are simply conveying information (for example, about a new book you have discovered) and have no investment in whether he uses the information. It would be ideal if you can work toward really *feeling* this way when you communicate information—no judgment, no investment.

Of course, if you tend to yell at your partner, you need to stop doing so. Yelling does absolutely no good and can even cause harm. It can undercut your partner's motivation and, perhaps most important, sabotage your attempts to develop a compassionate way of relating to him. If you yell at your partner because you have become discouraged and at that moment believe he will never change, you are being a disapproving parent or boss, not a supportive partner. You become the villain, and he focuses on how mean and out of control you are instead of on what you are trying to tell him or on how he could do something differently.

The bottom line: Harsh words will only make your partner feel guilt and shame, which in turn will decrease his motivation to change and even his belief that he can change. It will cause him to build up a defensive wall to keep you out and, in the process, make you the enemy, not a supportive partner.

AN ATTITUDE ADJUSTMENT

In order for your partner to begin to believe that you truly want to help him, you may need to work on your attitude as well as your behavior.

Situations are almost never black and white; it is unlikely as clear-cut as "he is the problem and I am the long-suffering partner." As we've discussed, codependent thinking and behavior can also be an addiction. And many experts believe that substance-dependent people and their partners have "parallel symptoms" or "parallel processes." The substance-dependent person becomes obsessed with their substance or behavior; their loved one becomes obsessed with their partner.

Some partners collude with their substance-dependent partner's denial and rationalization by making excuses for his behavior. Just as the substance abuser's tolerance for the addictive substance or behavior increases, so can his loved one's tolerance for her partner's behavior. And just as the substance-dependent partner isolates himself from the outside world, his partner tends to do the same.

So, the first thing you need to do is adjust your attitude. You are not your partner's savior, you are not morally superior to him, and you are not doing him a favor just by being with him. If you continue to view yourself this way—as a savior, a victim, or a martyr—your attempts to help him are not going to work. He will stay sick and so will you.

It is not a coincidence that you and your partner are together. You each have something to learn from one another, and you can each help the other learn your lessons. The most important thing you can do to support your partner in his recovery is to show that you are truly supportive and on his side. Begin to treat him with more kindness and respect, and communicate with him in a kinder, more respectful way (we'll talk more about how to do this in chapter 8). Stop trying to control him, and start giving him the space he needs to make his own mistakes and learn from them.

The bottom line: Your partner needs your compassion, not your contempt; he needs your support, not your pity; and he needs your acceptance, not your criticism.

CHAPTER 7

Should You Be a Supporter or a Collaborator?

"If everyone received the encouragement they need to grow, the genius in most everyone would blossom and the world would produce abundance beyond our wildest dreams."
—SIDNEY MADWED

SO FAR WE'VE TALKED ABOUT WHAT *NOT* TO DO TO HELP your partner on his road to recovery—shaming him, enabling him by fixing his mistakes or trying to protect him, using harsh words or tones that only lead to defensiveness. Now let's talk about what *to* do.

This chapter focuses on specific actions you can take by becoming either your partner's *supporter* or his *collaborator*, and which role is likely to be right for you and your partner. In either case, your goal is to bring out the best in your partner, not the worst. This will require an attitude of acceptance, understanding, and compassion. You want to let your partner know that you are behind him and that you trust him to know what he needs and what is going to work for him.

SUPPORTER OR COLLABORATOR: WHAT'S THE DIFFERENCE?

The primary difference between being your partner's supporter versus his collaborator is the degree of your involvement in his recovery process.

The role of supporter is more passive. In fact, you can be your partner's supporter without ever telling him you are doing so. All you need to do is engage in behavior that is supportive, encouraging, and compassionate as he works toward recovery.

The role of collaborator is more active and can be done only with your partner's agreement. It includes engaging in supportive behaviors but may also involve you and your partner sitting down together to discuss treatment options or even going as far as working together on a treatment plan.

Let's look at both of these roles in more detail, pulling together everything we've discussed so far.

Defining Supportive Behavior

Supportive behavior is any action on your part that will support your partner in his own efforts to recover. In most situations, it doesn't mean doing things for him, but rather letting go of control and allowing him to experience the consequences of his actions, learn from them, and make changes accordingly.

Supporting your partner doesn't involve nagging him to do things, criticizing him, blowing up, or giving him the silent treatment when he behaves badly. Instead, supportive behavior includes:

- *Getting out of his way.* This means not providing him with excuses to blame you for his substance problems and not sidetracking him in unproductive arguments or blaming sessions.

- *Staying connected to him.* The research is clear that partner and family involvement in helping a loved one struggling with substances increases the odds of improvement and helps maintain positive changes. Remaining connected allows you to be present to notice and reinforce his positive changes.

- *Treating him with patience, compassion, kindness, and respect.* Even if you have lost some respect for your partner because of his past behaviors, he still deserves to be treated with kindness and compassion.

- *Letting your partner know that you are on his side.* Show him by your words, your looks, and your actions that you are not his enemy; you are not trying to make him look or feel bad or trying to sabotage his efforts. You want him to heal, you want him to be happy, and you want him to succeed.

Defining Collaborative Behavior

To collaborate is to work together to perform a task and to achieve shared goals—in this case, your partner's recovery and the healing of your relationship. Working together collaboratively lets you access greater resources and therefore reap greater rewards.

In a collaborative relationship you are walking the path together, each doing your part. In this case, though you are working together toward your partner's recovery, you must still take your cues from him. After all, it is his journey.

Just as there is a fine but very distinct line between codependency and compassion, there is an equally fine but distinct line between enabling and being a collaborator. When we find ourselves trying to fix another person's problems or needing to help them for our own sense of identity, then we are enabling or rescuing. The message you want to relay is "I see you are doing well. Is there anything you need from me?" instead of "You're not doing it right. Here, do it this way!" or, even worse, "You're not doing it right. Let me do it."

In addition to the supportive behaviors already mentioned, here are some good examples of actions you can take as a collaborator:

- Agree to resolve potential problems and sticky situations together.

- Agree to practice techniques around reinforcement and consequences. (We'll outline some of these in chapter 8.)

- Learn all you can about the many treatment options. That way, if and when your partner is ready to talk about reaching out for help, you can offer him some suggestions. (For a detailed list of treatment options, refer to Appendix II.)

- Work with your partner to create a treatment plan that works for him.

DECIDING HOW YOU WILL HELP

Your decision to be a supporter or a collaborator doesn't have to be an either-or thing. Many of the suggestions for being a compassionate supporter also apply to being your partner's collaborator. And you might start out being a supporter and later decide with your partner that you should move into a collaborator role.

For now, focus on the role that seems right for you based on your present circumstances. Consider these elements to help you decide:

- *Your partner's willingness to include you in his recovery.* You may feel ready and able to be a full-fledged collaborator in your partner's recovery, but if he does not want your help, you will only be able to provide compassionate support from the sidelines. Some partners welcome their mate's active interest and participation in their recovery and some do not. It has to be his choice.

- *Your willingness and ability to focus on your own healing.* In other words, how much work do you need to do on yourself? Since your time and energy are limited, it makes no sense for you to devote yourself to his recovery if it means ignoring your own. If you have any of the important issues outlined in chapter 5 that you need to focus on, you may not be a good candidate to become a collaborator—but you can still be a great supporter.

- *How good you are at taking care of your own needs.* If you aren't doing a very good job of taking care of your own needs, you probably shouldn't try to focus on meeting the needs of your partner. Start by discovering which of your needs are unmet and on beginning to meet them; we'll give you some exercises to help with this in chapter 10. Once you are doing a better job of taking care of yourself, you can then revisit the idea of becoming your partner's collaborator.

Determining Your Willingness and Ability to Take Care of Your Own Needs

Many in the recovery movement believe that the primary way a loved one can help a substance abuser is to first take care of herself. In *Recover to Live,* Chris advises people in a relationship with an addict to "go take care of yourself and you will change everything . . . You have to focus on yourself. You must take care of yourself. When you do that, everything changes in the family system."[23]

But, as we've said here, there really is no one-size-fits-all solution when it comes to recovery for the substance-dependent person or his partner. Yes, it is important that you take care of yourself—vitally important. Yes, it is important that you address your own issues and eventually address your relationship dynamics. But you don't have to choose one or the other—to focus on yourself or to focus on your partner and your relationship. You can do both—really, all three—simultaneously.

Later in the book we'll look at how to begin addressing and healing your own issues. For now, the important question is whether you're proficient enough at basic self-care tasks, as well as self-nurturing and setting reasonable expectations for yourself, to be an effective collaborator. You can't expect your partner to meet all your needs for companionship, affection, or encouragement while he is focusing on his recovery. It will take all his energy and focus to continue struggling to rid himself of his substance dependence. If you can't give yourself what you need, trying to help your partner will only make things worse for you both.

> *Chris: Recovery has taught me that if I find something wrong in my world, I need to look at me. I had a sponsor in a twelve-step program who used to say to me, "I have only one problem in my life and I'm it." The first step toward helping your partner is to help yourself. You must put on your own life jacket first if you want any hope of saving him or yourself. If you stay without treating your own issues and initiating your own recovery, you will both drown in misery. If your partner has an active addiction—if he's already in the deep end—throw him a rope, but don't get in with him. He'll pull you down.*

{EXERCISE}

A SELF-CARE ASSESSMENT

Write *True* or *False* for each item.

1. I am aware of what I am feeling at any given time.
2. I am numb to my feelings a great deal of the time.
3. I am able to recognize and meet my needs.
4. I am not able to recognize my needs, so I cannot meet them.
5. I am able to ask for help from others.
6. I remain isolated from others and cannot ask for help.
7. I set goals for myself that are reasonable, based on my capabilities.
8. I set unreasonable expectations for myself.
9. I am aware of a safe place inside me.
10. I feel empty, numb, or lost a great deal of the time.
11. My inner voice is nurturing and warm.
12. My inner voice is critical and demanding.
13. When life is hard, I soothe myself from within.
14. When life is hard, I soothe myself with food, alcohol, drugs, or other external "solutions."
15. I can feel the pain of the past and let it go.
16. I shut out my bad feelings about the past.
17. I am physically active.
18. I resist physical activity.
19. I eat a healthy diet.
20. My diet is not healthy.
21. I take time to restore my body, mind, and spirit.
22. I continue to push myself to do, do, do.

Take a look at your answers to the odd-numbered statements. If you answered "true" to most of these questions, you are doing a good job of taking care of yourself.

If you answered "false" to many of the odd-numbered questions and "true" to many of the even-numbered questions, taking care of yourself is something you struggle with, and it probably would not be a good idea for you to become your partner's collaborator at this time.

Former victims of abuse or neglect are especially at risk of becoming disconnected from or numb to their feelings and needs. They may not feed themselves when their body needs fuel because they are numb to the feelings of hunger. They may not allow themselves to cry or to seek out someone to talk to because they do not recognize when they are feeling sad or lonely. For this reason, if you are a former victim of abuse or neglect, exercise extra caution when it comes to choosing to be your partner's collaborator.

When It Isn't Possible for You to Be His Collaborator

In addition to self-care issues, there are specific cases in which it may not be possible for you to become your partner's collaborator and will require you to remain in the role of supporter. These can include:

- When your partner refuses to admit that he has a problem.

- When your partner's behavior triggers an extreme negative reaction in you, either because of childhood issues or because of strong moral beliefs on your part (for example, if he is addicted to porn and you are a victim of sexual abuse or against pornography of any kind).

- When your partner's behavior gets in the way of your own recovery (for example, you have been clean and sober for years but your husband's increased use of alcohol leaves you resentful).

Beverly's client Janet is a good example of someone who could not be a collaborator because of the way her partner's behavior intersected with her own childhood issues:

> I've recently discovered that my husband is addicted to pornography—the kind you can access on the internet. I feel so embarrassed about even saying that. And when I think about him watching that garbage it makes me feel physically ill. I felt betrayed.

Janet caught her husband watching it one night when she got up to go to the bathroom. When she confronted him he told her the pornography had come up automatically. But because she had watched a TV program on pornography, Janet knew this couldn't be true. Her husband finally admitted that he had gone on a site and that he used it as a form of stress reduction so he could relax and go to sleep.

A few days later, once Janet had calmed down, she talked with her husband about other ways he could handle stress. She asked him if he had a problem with the frequency of sex between them, and he assured her that he was happy with their sex life and that there was no problem between them. He also promised he would stop viewing porn, but she later checked his history on the computer and discovered he had continued. She went ballistic and told him that unless he stopped she would end the relationship.

> He knows I was sexually abused as a child and that just the thought of pornography pushes all my buttons. The thought of him watching it makes him repulsive to me—almost the way I feel when I think of a child molester. The whole thing feels sleazy to me—him watching it and masturbating to the images, and hiding it from me—it is just too close to the associations I have with sexual abuse.
>
> I'm sorry to say that I've lost respect for him and I no longer trust him. I don't know if I can believe what he says anymore, and I'm not even sure if he's doing other things behind my back. I just don't feel I can live with this.

As Beverly explained to Janet, sometimes it doesn't matter how much you love your partner, no matter how much compassion and understanding you have for him, there can be a limit as to what you are willing or capable of doing.

Although not in a formal way, Janet had actually started out being a compassionate collaborator with her husband. She had the right idea when she talked to him about finding alternative ways of relieving his stress. This is actually one of the first steps to creating a collaborative relationship with your partner—talking about reasons for the dependency and discussing other ways to meet his needs.

It was also a good idea for her to inquire about whether their sex life was fulfilling for him. Partners tend to take the compulsive behavior of their partners personally, so it's good to check it out. If he had told her there was a problem, it could have opened the door to working on their sexual relationship.

But while Janet had good intentions and had even taken some positive steps toward collaborating with her husband on his problem, her own issues were getting in the way. Try as she might, she couldn't get past her repulsion toward him or the sense of betrayal she felt since he knew how his continued behavior affected her.

In other words, her own issues prevented her from having compassion for her partner—compassion that was necessary if she was going to be able to help him. Janet would have had to essentially sacrifice her own health and well-being in order to support her husband in his recovery.

Even though Janet's husband had agreed to go into psychotherapy to figure out why he had become compulsive about pornography, this didn't help Janet much. She had lost so much trust in him that she didn't feel optimistic about him being honest enough in therapy for him to really get help.

Beverly advised Janet to continue therapy, either with her or with someone else, in order to help her work through her feelings of anger, humiliation, betrayal, and pain. She also needed a safe place to continue processing the sexual abuse she had experienced at the hands of her grandfather when she was a child, a man she had also loved and trusted but who had betrayed her trust.

Eventually, Janet was able to separate her feelings for her grandfather from her feelings toward her husband. Still, she could not tolerate her husband's behavior. Since they had children and she didn't want to disrupt their lives, Janet decided to tell her husband that for the time being he had to sleep in their guest room. She made it clear that she could not sleep in the same bed with him and that she certainly could not have sex with him. Because of the circumstances, it was clear Janet would not at any point be able to collaborate with her husband in his recovery.

Can You Be "All In"?

The final consideration in choosing to be your partner's collaborator versus his supporter is whether you can be "all in."

Being all in means that you have considered the situation very carefully and have committed to staying with your partner and helping him with his recovery. It's okay if you can make that commitment for only a certain amount of time, such as six months or a year, but you do need to commit. If you go into this process feeling defeated and assuming it is not going to work (because nothing has before), or questioning whether you can actually help, that negativity can doom both your and your partner's efforts from the beginning. Your partner needs to know that you feel optimistic about the process—and that you believe in him.

Being all in also requires you to take a hiatus from arguing, coercing, blaming, and other behaviors that often become habit for partners of substance- or activity-dependent people. You can't expect your partner to believe that you are a compassionate collaborator who is there to support him if you are angry, impatient, or critical.

This doesn't mean that you won't get angry along the way when he fails to keep a commitment or when he slips into old behaviors. What it means is that you learn to express your disappointment, anger, and frustration in more constructive ways, away from him, and that you take responsibility for your feelings by practicing the methods of release in the next chapter.

Now that we've discussed what role you are going to play in your partner's recovery—supporter or collaborator—let's look more closely at some strategies for each.

CHAPTER 8

Becoming a Compassionate Supporter

IF YOU HAVE DECIDED TO BE YOUR PARTNER'S SUPPORTER, THIS chapter will give you specific strategies to help you do so. But even if you have decided to become your partner's collaborator, don't skip ahead; the advice and strategies here will be very helpful to you. Think of this chapter as a primer or introduction for becoming a collaborator.

If you have decided, for whatever reason, that it is best for you and your partner if you don't attempt to work directly with him as his collaborator, this chapter will guide you in becoming a compassionate supporter. We will share ways to create a compassionate environment—one that supports your partner emotionally. You will learn how to (1) view your partner in a more compassionate way, (2) express your anger in constructive ways instead of taking it out on your partner, and (3) minimize or even eliminate shaming behaviors. We will also teach you how to become more self-compassionate, since the more compassion you feel for yourself, the more you'll have for your partner.

CREATING A COMPASSIONATE ENVIRONMENT

By creating a compassionate environment around your partner, you encourage him to come out of denial by making him feel safer and more secure, which in turn will help him take the steps—and the risks—necessary to recover.

You can create this environment in several ways:

- *Soothe your partner's hurts and comfort his pain.* Even if your partner does not share his suffering with you (or even denies he is suffering), an understanding look, a sigh, or a comforting touch can still communicate that *you are with him in his pain.* As we discussed in chapter 3, this expression of compassion from you will help him feel less alone in his struggle to recover.

- *Work on being more empathetic toward your partner.* In other words, put yourself in his place and imagine how he feels. As impatient, disappointed, and angry at your partner as you sometimes feel, imagine how he must feel about himself. Yes, he may act as though he doesn't care; he may become defensive and deny he has a problem. But beneath the wall he has built up, he is feeling deeply impatient, disappointed, and angry with himself. And he is feeling deeply ashamed of himself. (This is why it is so important for you to avoid shaming him further—we'll discuss this later.)

- *Provide the space for your partner to share his suffering with you* by not constantly complaining about how much you suffer because of him and his substance abuse. He is unlikely to feel open to admitting how much he suffers if he is constantly on the defensive, warding off attacks. (We'll provide ways for you to release your anger later on in this chapter.)

- *Work on understanding your partner's substance dependence*—including what caused it, and why it is so difficult to break. It is harder to have compassion for someone when we don't understand why they behave as they do. You began this work in chapter 4, but we encourage you to continue it.

- *Provide compassion for yourself.* The more compassionate you are with yourself about how you are suffering, the more compassionate you will be able to be with your partner. (We'll offer you suggestions for how to go about this later on in this chapter as well.)

COMMON OBSTACLES TO CREATING A COMPASSIONATE ENVIRONMENT

No one said that creating a compassionate environment would be easy. And no matter how much you like the idea or how eager you are to begin creating this kind of environment, chances are there will be some obstacles in your way.

In order to create a compassionate environment you first need to feel compassionate toward your partner. Having compassion for someone means that you are moved by his pain, that you join him in his suffering, and that you feel the urge to help him in some way.

In general, those who have codependent tendencies sometimes have *too much* empathy or compassion for others, meaning that they think of others' needs before their own, feel their partners' suffering too much, and blur the boundaries between themselves and others, making others' suffering their own. But you may still have a difficult time having compassion for your partner. You may feel compassion for those you consider to be blameless victims but have difficulty feeling it for those whose suffering stems from failures, personal weaknesses, or bad decisions. Instead of feeling compassion for your partner, you may close your heart to his suffering, telling yourself that he has brought it on himself.

If you have difficulty feeling your partner's feelings, it can help to draw an association between your partner and yourself. The next time you see that your partner is suffering, try to remember a time when you suffered in a similar way.

Another strategy for increasing feelings of compassion toward your partner is to work on your self-compassion. Self-compassion is key to becoming more compassionate toward others, as it's difficult to feel for your partner something you don't feel for yourself. (We'll offer more information on how to develop more self-compassion later in this chapter.)

Other frequent obstacles to creating a compassionate environment include:

1. Displaying anger toward your partner

2. Shaming your partner

3. Feeling sorry for yourself

4. Taking your partner's behavior personally

Let's discuss each of these obstacles, and how to get past them, in more detail.

Displaying Anger toward Your Partner

The first and probably most powerful obstacle is anger and resentment toward your partner. After all, it is highly likely that you have been deeply hurt by your partner's behavior. Things he has done (or left undone) have significantly affected your life and, if you have children, your children's lives. Your partner has probably let you down in very painful ways, and you may feel deeply disappointed and betrayed.

In spite of your love for your partner, and in spite of your desire to help him, these feelings of resentment, anger, hurt, and betrayal can get in the way of experiencing compassion for him and creating the kind of environment you want to create. For this reason it is important for you to find a way to release this anger so that you can focus on being his supporter (or collaborator).

Consider any or all of the following healthy, constructive ways to vent your anger, depending on what speaks to you most:

- Write a letter to your partner that you will not give to him. In the letter, tell him exactly how his substance abuse has affected you. Don't hold back; let all your feelings of anger and hurt come out on the page. You may want to burn the letter or tear it up into tiny pieces afterward as a symbolic gesture of getting rid of your anger.

- When you are alone at home, talk out loud to yourself, expressing all the angry feelings you are having. Don't censor yourself; say exactly what is on your mind in whatever kind of language you choose.

- Imagine you are sitting across from your partner. Now imagine telling him exactly how his addiction has negatively affected you. Again, don't hold back and don't censor yourself.

- Put your face in a pillow and scream as you think about how difficult your life has been for you thanks to your partner's addiction.

- If you feel as though you need to release your anger physically, ask your body what it needs to do. You might get the sense that you need to hit, kick, push, break things, or tear things up. Honor that intuitive feeling by finding a way to do so in a safe but satisfying way—for example, kneeling down next to your bed and hitting it with your fists. If you are alone and no one is around, you can let out sounds as you hit. You can lie on your bed and kick your legs, or you can stomp on egg cartons or other packaging; you can tear up old telephone books, or go to a deserted place and throw rocks or bottles.

Know, also, that releasing your anger is an ongoing process, not a one-time thing. You have, no doubt, built up a tremendous mountain of anger over the years; getting rid of it will take time. Think of each episode of anger release as taking one more boulder off that mountain.

If you have difficulty giving yourself permission to get angry or fear losing control if you do so, refer to Beverly's book *Honor Your Anger*.

Shaming Your Partner

One of the most powerful things you can do to support your partner in his recovery is to stop shaming him.

First, there is scientific evidence that shaming doesn't work when it comes to changing someone's behavior, and in fact causes more harm than good. Keep in mind that few people change in response to shame. When we shame someone, we alienate and isolate him, which tends to make him feel disconnected. The shamed person becomes angry and feels terrible about himself. An angry, disconnected person who hates himself has little motivation to change and is far more likely to continue his addictive behavior.

Second, as we've discussed, your partner is likely to be overwhelmed with shame already. Humiliating him further, making him out to be a selfish monster, will only cause him to remain defensive.

THE RELATIONSHIP BETWEEN ALCOHOLISM AND SHAME

Jessica Tracy and Daniel Randles at the University of British Columbia conducted a study to discover whether alcoholics' feelings of shame about their addiction might actually interfere with their attempts to get sober. They recruited about a hundred women and men from AA meeting rooms—all with less than six months of sobriety—and measured their levels of shame and other emotions, along with certain personality traits.

One reason shame has gone unstudied is that it is a very difficult emotion to capture. People who are experiencing shame tend to hide it and escape it, not talk about it openly. Tracy and Randles decided to measure the level of shame by noting participants' body language. They asked their volunteers to describe the last time they drank and "felt bad about it." They then videotaped their responses. Later, they analyzed and coded the volunteers' body movements and postures as a measure of their shameful feelings. People who were ashamed act very much like submissive animals, slumping their shoulders and narrowing their chest. This physical display of shame may be universal, as it has been observed in both adults and children in many cultures.

The scientists wanted to see whether this shameful body language correlated with mental and physical health and especially with successful sobriety four months later—the window of time in which most newly recovered alcoholics will relapse. Indeed, more than half of the volunteers never made it back to the lab at the four-month checkpoint. But for those who did, the researchers noted an unmistakable connection between shame and relapse. The alcoholics who were most ashamed about their last drink—typically a humiliating experience—were more likely to relapse. Their relapses were also more severe, involving much more drinking, and they were more likely to suffer other declines in health.

In short, feelings of shame do not appear to promote sobriety or protect against future problematic drinking—indeed, the opposite appears to be true.

This is the first scientific evidence to bolster what alcoholism counselors and recovering alcoholics have long known: *Shame is a core emotion underlying chronic heavy drinking.* Shame is what gets people into the rooms of AA—it defines the alcoholic "bottom"—but it's not a good motivator for staying in recovery. The power of AA is that it offers something positive to replace that negative emotion that most alcoholics know all too intimately.[24]

How to Stop Adding to His Stockpile of Shame

To create a compassionate environment, it is very important that you not add to your partner's stockpile of shame. Shaming your partner only makes him feel worse about himself. Since your goal is to support him, you want to do everything you can to help him feel better about himself, not the opposite.

Letting go of shaming behavior can be difficult. It probably has become a habit—a way for you to release your frustration and anger at his behavior. But as you work on releasing your anger toward your partner in more constructive ways, you will find that you are less likely to want to shame your partner, which will make that habit easier to break.

In order to break the shaming habit, begin to notice how often you shame him with statements such as these:

- "I can't believe you did it again. You promised me you wouldn't. You have absolutely no willpower, do you?"

- "When are you going to grow up and start acting like a man?

- "You're such a loser."

- "You're a hopeless case. I feel sorry for you."

- "I don't know why I stay with you. God knows no other woman would put up with this kind of crap!"

- "What's wrong with you? You're pathetic! Can't you control yourself for even one day?"

When you catch yourself saying something shaming to your partner, take a moment and ask yourself, "What am I feeling right now? Why do I feel the need to shame my partner?" It may simply be that shaming him has become a habit—but that habit likely originated as a way for you to vent your anger or frustration or to avoid feeling deeper feelings of disappointment or hurt.

Feeling Sorry for Yourself

One reason for your anger at your partner and your tendency to shame him is that you desire validation and appreciation for all *you* have suffered because of his substance abuse.

Unfortunately, you are not likely to get this kind of validation from your partner. First of all, he probably feels too defensive or too ashamed to give it to you. Second, it is likely that your partner did not receive compassion or validation as a child and therefore doesn't know how to give these things to others.

Other people may not be very forthcoming when it comes to offering you compassion, either. Friends and family may have advised you to leave your partner, and since you haven't done so, they might have grown impatient with you. Or perhaps they are in denial about just how serious your partner's problems are and expect you to stay with him no matter how bad it gets, offering no understanding for how much you have suffered.

It comes down to this: You need to provide for yourself the validation and compassion you need and deserve.

In addition to being the best way you can support your partner, compassion is the most powerful tool you have for helping yourself as you take on the role of supporter or collaborator. Self-compassion will help you remain strong even in the most difficult of times. It will help you bounce back from your partner's inappropriate, embarrassing, hurtful, or abusive behavior. Most important, self-compassion will help motivate you to take care of yourself. Self-compassion encourages us to begin to talk to and treat ourselves with the same kindness and caring we would show a good friend or a beloved child.

SELF-COMPASSION DEFINED

If compassion is the ability to feel and connect with the suffering of another human being, self-compassion is the ability to feel and connect with *one's own suffering*. Kristin Neff, professor of psychology at the University of Texas at Austin, is the leading researcher in the growing field of self-compassion. In her book *Self-Compassion*, she defines self-compassion as "being open to and moved by one's own suffering, experiencing feelings of caring and kindness toward oneself, taking an understanding, nonjudgmental attitude toward one's inadequacies and failures, and recognizing that one's experience is part of the common human experience."[25]

If we are to be self-compassionate, we need to give ourselves the same gifts we offer to others for whom we express compassion. In other words, we need to offer ourselves the same *recognition*, *validation*, and *support* we would offer a loved one who is suffering.

Most of us were raised to persevere despite difficulties. And while persevering is important, it's also essential that we not ignore our feelings about how difficult something is, but rather acknowledge that difficulty and have compassion for it.

Stopping to acknowledge your suffering with self-compassion is not the same as whining, wallowing in self-pity, or feeling sorry for yourself. When we are experiencing self-pity we tend to complain, to ourselves and others, about how bad a situation is, while seeing ourselves as helpless to change it. There is often a bitter tone to our thoughts and feelings. Being angry about a situation or about what someone did to hurt you is fine, and even healing; it is when you allow bitterness and helplessness to cause you to dwell on how you've been victimized that you get stuck in self-pity.

If you are a partner of someone who has a substance abuse problem, you have suffered. There's no denying that you've been hurt and embarrassed and angered by your partner's behavior. You may have lost friends and money, your career may have suffered, and your health may have been affected since you have likely suffered both emotionally and physically. But self-pity doesn't help you, and it can also prevent you from helping your partner. Self-compassion, on the other hand, helps you both.

Thinking and acting with self-compassion has been shown to have psychological benefits, including the reduction of negative feelings, such as distress, and increased well-being, optimism, and happiness.[26]

Two of Beverly's clients, with very similar circumstances, made the following two statements:

1. "My whole life has been ruined by my husband's alcoholism. We don't have any friends anymore because he's managed to anger or insult everyone. Our kids don't bring their friends over anymore because they are too ashamed of him. I should leave him, but when he's sober he's a really good father. The whole situation just seems hopeless. I just feel angry and stuck. I resent him for putting me in this position."

2. "I feel sad when I think of what my husband's alcoholism has done to our family. The kids are embarrassed to bring anyone to the house, and most of our friends have

become alienated from us because of his behavior. I feel stuck because I think I should leave him, but he is a good husband and father when he's sober. I guess it is understandable that I would feel so stuck. After all, it is a difficult situation with no easy answers. I think I need some help so I can decide what to do."

The woman in the first example is feeling a lot of resentment and bitterness. She seems to feel hopeless and to blame her husband for her own confusion about what to do. The tone of her statement is self-pitying.

The woman in the second example also seems to feel hopeless, but she acknowledges that she feels sad, too. Her statement displays self-compassion. In it, she acknowledges her feelings, and this in itself can help her begin to feel better. Using the phrase "it is understandable" validates her experience without blaming herself or her husband.

Where the first woman is focused on saying "poor me," the second woman, having validated her feelings, is focused outward on how she can get help.

Self-compassion can also lead to more proactive behavior. Once you've validated your feelings and your experience, you may feel motivated to improve your situation. Beverly often finds this to be the case with people who are currently being either emotionally or physically abused. Once they acknowledge their suffering and allow themselves to feel and express their emotions about the abuse, they often feel more impetus to leave the relationship.

Just as connecting with the suffering of others has been shown to comfort and heal, connecting with our own suffering will do the same. The more you provide for yourself the compassion you so desperately need, the less inclined you will be to continually remind your partner of how much he has disappointed, embarrassed, and hurt you or how he has ruined his life. This is a crucial step toward creating a compassionate environment.

If you'd like to find out how self-compassionate you already are, go to www.self-compassion.org and take the quiz. The site also offers some self-compassion practices you can perform in addition to the exercise below.

{EXERCISE}
BECOMING COMPASSIONATE TOWARD YOURSELF

Think about the most compassionate person you have known—someone kind, understanding, and supportive of you. It may have been a teacher, a friend, a friend's parent, or a relative. Think about how this person conveyed compassion toward you and how you felt in this person's presence. Notice the feelings and sensations that come up with this memory. If you can't think of someone in your life who has been compassionate toward you, think of a compassionate public figure, or even a fictional character from a book, film, or television show.

Now imagine that you have the ability to become as compassionate toward yourself as this person has been toward you (or as you imagine this person would be toward you). See if you can single out what this person did that made you feel so cared about: the words, gestures, looks, or touches. Now use these to help you provide for yourself the things this person provided for you. Try talking to yourself in the same way, or using the same loving words or soothing tones. If the person physically comforted you, repeat this gesture toward yourself.

Taking Your Partner's Behavior Personally

It can be difficult to not take your partner's behavior personally. When he lies to you or blames you, it feels insulting and disrespectful. When he doesn't come home, it feels as if he doesn't care how worried you become. *If he loved me*, you may think, *he wouldn't continue to abuse alcohol* (or gamble, or use pornography). But it is vital that you understand, and remind yourself whenever needed, that his inappropriate, hurtful, or abusive behavior most likely doesn't say anything about how he feels about you. It does, however, say everything about how he feels about himself.

Your partner isn't using because of you—because he's trying to punish you, or because he wants to get even with you, or because he hates you. He may at times give these *excuses* for using, but they aren't true. His dependence problems stem from his own issues and problems, not from who you are or even how he feels about you.

This may sound like a contradiction, because we are saying that your partner's substance abuse doesn't have anything to do with you, yet we are also telling you that your behavior can influence whether or not he stops using. The difference is this: While shaming him may cause him to become more defensive and less motivated, and may even give him an excuse in the moment to use, his compulsion to use a substance or an activity comes from deep inside himself. This compulsion is an attempt to soothe or take away the excruciating pain inside him, pain most likely originating in childhood trauma. If you stop shaming him, he won't have that as an excuse to use and may have to look inside himself to discover the real reason he uses.

MORE SUPPORTIVE STRATEGIES

It can take time and sometimes hard work to move past the obstacles in the way of creating a compassionate environment. But if you continue to work at it, following the advice and strategies offered here, you will find that you have created a supportive space that will benefit both you and your partner.

Still, creating a compassionate environment that encourages change is just one strategy for supporting your partner. Being supportive also involves *looking at things through your partner's perspective* instead of only your own. This includes beginning to trust that even if you don't agree with some of your partner's choices regarding his recovery, you need to step back and *allow him to be in charge of his own process.*

There are many legitimate paths to recovery, and your partner knows what will work for him better than you do. Although many people respond well to twelve-step programs like Alcoholics Anonymous or Narcotics Anonymous, these programs don't work for everyone. If your partner knows this about himself, you can support him by not trying to talk him into it. Offering options (instead of ultimatums) is a positive way to support him, but so is trusting that he will find the right option for himself. There is even evidence showing that there's a good chance that your partner can get better without treatment, if he's properly motivated. One national survey found that 24 percent of people diagnosed with alcohol dependence—the most severe category of alcohol problem—recovered *on their own within a year.*[27]

Being supportive also includes these strategies:

- *Have supportive conversations* in which you openly listen when he feels remorse or guilt for what his substance dependence has caused him to do.

- *Encourage him to face the truth about his behavior.* This means that you do not "comfort" him by telling him things are not that bad. If he is feeling guilt or remorse for what he has done, this is a positive thing; it is when he recognizes the consequences of his substance dependency that he is closest to making a decision to change or to reach out for help. However, be sure that, while doing this, you also . . .

- *Encourage him when he's down.* If he begins shaming himself with statements like "I'm a loser" or "I'm worthless" or "I don't deserve you and the kids," don't let him go on for too long. Listen compassionately when he is looking at his problems more realistically, and after he's shared with you how bad he feels, say something supportive about him and his ability to change.

This is what Beverly's client Judy said to her husband, who was recovering from a drug dependence, when he began to shame himself about his behavior in front of their children the last time he'd been high:

Yes, it is true that you've embarrassed the kids, and this has caused them to lose respect for you. I can understand that knowing this is really painful. But I believe you can turn this thing around. I know you and I know how strong you are. If you really want to change, I know you can and I will be here every step of the way to encourage you. If you want we can talk about what options there are for treatment.

Judy's statement didn't negate what he'd done to hurt others, which is important. But instead of allowing him to shame himself, Judy *expressed empathy and compassion* with the words "I can understand." She focused on his *feelings* versus letting him call himself names or demean himself. Then she offered support and encouragement in the form of letting him know she believed in him and believed he could change. Finally she offered to help in a concrete way, by talking about options.

- *Continue to change the way you think about substance use and compulsive behavior.* The more you understand about substance dependence, the more you will be able to change your way of thinking about it and become more compassionate and understanding and less critical and judgmental. We provided a great deal of information in chapter 4, but we also recommend you do some further reading, such as Chris's book *Recover to Live*, and *Beyond Addiction* by Jeffrey Foote, Carrie Wilkens, and Nicole Kosanke.

- *Understand why your partner uses.* Gaining a better understanding of what benefits the substance or compulsive behavior provides him will help you have more empathy toward him. It may also help you identify how you can modify your behavior, your relationship, and the environment to better support his long-term change. (We provide more information and an exercise to help with this in the next chapter.)

- *Learn all you can about what motivates a person to change.* Put simply: *Motivation for change occurs whenever the costs of a behavior perceptibly outweigh the benefits.* While you can't motivate your partner to change, by understanding his motivations better— both his motivation to use substances, as discussed above, and his motivation to change—you can better support him when he is motivated. Understanding his motivation will also help you avoid feeling excessive disappointment when he wavers in his attempts to change. (We provide a strategy to learn more about your partner's motivations in the next chapter. There is also an excellent section on motivation in *Beyond Addiction*.)

- *Understand that when you help yourself, you help your partner.* Be as willing to change your own unhealthy attitudes and behaviors as you want your partner to be. By taking care of your physical and emotional health, by improving your resilience, and by putting social supports in place, you not only set a good example but also ensure you have the internal and external resources you'll need to successfully help your partner. (See chapter 10 for more information about self-care.)

WHAT YOU CAN'T DO

In order to fully support your partner, you need to know not just what you can do, but also what you *can't* do, if you want to help him. Remind yourself that:

1. You can't change your partner.
2. You can't make your partner want to change.

What you can do is help your partner realize that he wants to change by helping reduce his need to defend his current behavior.

{EXERCISE}

YOUR PLAN FOR BEING YOUR PARTNER'S SUPPORTER

Refer to all the information we've shared so far and write up a personal plan of action using the suggestions that most resonate with you. For example, you may see your role as his supporter consisting of being less judgmental and more compassionate toward him, being his "cheerleader," and working on not taking his dependency issues personally.

Remember: Often, what looks like an unwillingness to change is a defensive stance. Those with substance problems respond with significantly less resistance when they are treated with kindness, compassion, and respect. Your job as your partner's compassionate supporter is to provide those things.

This in itself is an enormous task, and you need to give yourself a great deal of self-acknowledgment for attempting it. It's also a role that should not be minimized. Although your partner's recovery is ultimately his responsibility, he desperately needs your support and encouragement if he is going to be successful.

CHAPTER 9

Becoming a
Compassionate Collaborator

YOU'VE DECIDED THAT YOU ARE IN A GOOD PLACE EMOTION-
ally to become your partner's collaborator (you regularly practice self-care, and your partner's substance dependence does not get in the way of your own recovery process). You've also read the previous chapter on creating a supportive environment. Your partner has admitted that he has a problem and is open to your help.

The next step is discussing with him the idea of you becoming his collaborator. Make sure that both you and your partner are making a free choice to begin this process—that neither of you is doing it out of obligation. Don't decide to become his collaborator because you "owe it to him" as his partner. And he doesn't "owe it to you" to try this because you have put up with so much from him. Be careful that you do not emotionally blackmail him into agreeing by subtly suggesting (or overtly announcing) that this is his last chance and that you will leave him if he doesn't cooperate, or that doing this is the only way to prove that he loves you.

You can ask him to read this book, as well as *Beyond Addiction*, or simply explain the process of becoming his collaborator. Once he understands what you're suggesting, ask him how he feels about it.

If he immediately rejects the idea, ask him in a nondemanding way what turns him off about it. If he is willing and able to explain his reasons to you, listen without making any comments. One of your roles, as collaborator *or* supporter, is to try to understand his position. Once he is finished, and only if he seems open to it, see if you can explain the concept to him in a way that is less threatening and even inviting. If he still doesn't like the idea, drop it for now. There may be another time when he seems more open to it and, as detailed in the previous chapter, there are ways you can begin to support him even without his cooperation.

If he likes the idea of you being his collaborator, ask him how he envisions you playing this role. Asking for his ideas first—as opposed to beginning with your own—is in fact a good example of collaborative behavior on your part. Give him time to think instead of pressuring him for answers. In the meantime, work on becoming more patient (one of the skills of being supportive). By giving him time, you will probably get a fairly good sense as to whether he is enthusiastic about the idea or has concerns. If you sense he is ambivalent, invite him to talk about his concerns and listen openly. Don't try to persuade him or argue with him.

If he doesn't get back to you at all, don't nag him; instead, ask him if he needs more time to think about it, if he forgot about it, or if he has decided he doesn't really like the idea. Make sure you do this with a good attitude and without sighing, eye rolling, whining, or self-pity.

If your partner comes back with some ideas about how he'd like you to collaborate with him on his recovery, acknowledge his willingness by first simply listening without comment. Some of his ideas may strike you as foolish or may sound too "enabling," but just hear him out. One of your roles as his collaborator is to help him bring out the best in himself. So, don't shut him down, no matter what he says. Often, what sounds like a bad idea may become a good one if your partner is allowed to explore it freely. Try to find something in what he shared with you to respond to in a positive light. For example: "I really loved your idea about ＿＿. Can you tell me more about why you think it might help you?" While an idea may have sounded ridiculous to you initially, his answer might change your mind, or the two of you might be able to work together to discover a way to tweak his idea into something more workable.

CREATE A COLLABORATION AGREEMENT

In order to facilitate the collaboration between you and your partner, we encourage you to create a Collaboration Agreement. This agreement should include the following details:

- How much assistance your partner wants and needs
- How you will offer that assistance
- How to determine when that assistance is no longer needed

In creating this agreement, you and your partner will need to work together, using both of your ideas. You may even find it helpful to actually write out your agreement so there are no disagreements in the future as to what your role is.

Although you need to allow him to be the leader in the discussion, do not agree to anything you are uncomfortable with. For example, Beverly's client Roger wanted his wife Jasmine to tell him two positive things about himself every day in order to make up for all the negative things he felt she had said about him in the past. He thought this would help raise his self-esteem. At first Jasmine thought this sounded like a good idea, but after thinking about it for a while she realized she wasn't comfortable with it. First of all, it felt to her as if she was being made to "pay" for her previous comments. Second, she felt it wasn't her role to raise his self-esteem—it was his.

Jasmine explained these reasons to him, adding that it didn't feel "organic" to have to come up with two items every day. She felt too much pressure to have to do so on demand. Instead, she promised to tell him more often when she was feeling good about him or about something he had done. This seemed to satisfy Roger.

Here is the text of Roger and Jasmine's Collaboration Agreement:

We agree to work together to help Roger be successful in his efforts to reach recovery from alcohol abuse. This means that instead of remaining in an adversarial relationship, we will work together as allies in a joint effort against the real enemy—alcohol dependence.

In order to make the most of our collaborative efforts, Jasmine agrees to do the following:

- Stop accusing, interrogating, and scolding Roger about his drinking behavior.
- Instead, tell Roger how she feels when he is drinking (sad, disappointed, angry) and how much happier she is when he is not.
- Stop rolling her eyes, being sarcastic, and making fun of Roger in front of their friends.
- Understand that slips are part of the recovery process, so don't berate Roger when he messes up and drinks.
- Recognize that Roger is doing the best he can to change his behavior.
- Have compassion for how difficult it is for Roger to stop drinking.

In turn, Roger agrees to do the following:

- Work with Jasmine to create a "recovery plan" in order to make stopping drinking more doable.
- Sit down with Jasmine periodically and talk about what is working and what isn't.
- Work on being less defensive about his drinking and more honest when he has slipped.
- Talk openly with Jasmine about what triggers slips and brainstorm together on how to deal with being triggered in the future.

HOW DO I KNOW IF I'M BEING COLLABORATIVE?

You may not always feel certain that you are being collaborative and helpful in the way you are speaking to your partner, the suggestions you are making, the things you are doing, or even the way you are thinking about a problem. When this happens, ask yourself the following questions:

- Do my words or actions communicate empathy?
- Am I trying to acknowledge, understand, and accept my partner as he is, not how I wish he was?
- Am I offering information or am I pushing it on him?
- Am I remembering that there is always more than one option?
- Am I respecting my partner's ability (and right) to choose what is best for him?
- Have I considered his point of view?
- Am I treating him as if I believe in him and his ability to change?
- Am I giving him positive feedback for positive behavior?[28]

In chapter 6 we introduced you to Marlene and Dan. Dan wanted to go to his friend's bachelor party in Atlantic City even though he was a compulsive gambler in recovery; Marlene thought it was too risky for him to go. Here is how Marlene and Dan dealt with the problem in a collaborative way.

Marlene started the conversation with "I understand how important it is that you go to support your friend Jim, and you acknowledge that it will be difficult for you not to gamble while in Atlantic City. So, what ideas can we come up with to help you resist the urge to gamble while you are there?"

Together, they came up with four ideas:

1. Dan will call Marlene to check in while in Atlantic City.
2. Dan will not drink too much alcohol while there since alcohol impairs his judgment.
3. Dan agrees to limit the amount of money he has access to while in Atlantic City.
4. Marlene will meet Dan in Atlantic City after the bachelor party for a couple's retreat.

This collaborative effort on both their parts turned out to be successful. Dan called Marlene every evening just before he was to meet up with his friends. He had agreed to do this (and wasn't coerced by Marlene) because he suspected that touching base with her would help him feel connected to her and remind him of the new life they were building together.

Checking in with Marlene also encouraged him to take his "emotional temperature" to discover how he was feeling about himself and the situation. One night during their call, Dan realized that he wasn't feeling emotionally strong. He was extremely tired and had been drinking too much, and it was catching up with him. While on the phone with Marlene, he decided not to meet his friends that night but to go to bed early instead. He reported waking up the next day feeling refreshed, strong, and confident in his ability to take care of himself. In the past he would have ignored his own needs and feelings and pushed himself to meet his friends so he wouldn't disappoint them.

Knowing that Marlene was going to meet him after the bachelor party for a couple's retreat gave Dan something to look forward to whenever he began to feel deprived because he wasn't gambling. He spent quite a lot of time planning what they would do when she arrived and making special arrangements to surprise her—a positive alternative to spending his time feeling sorry for himself.

THREE RECOMMENDED COLLABORATIVE STRATEGIES

In chapter 3 we introduced CRAFT (Community Reinforcement and Family Training), a scientifically supported, evidence-based, clinically proven approach to helping families cope with and support substance-dependent family members.

CRAFT's program has three goals: (1) to teach partners and family members skills to take care of themselves, (2) to teach them skills they can use to help their loved one change, and (3) to reduce substance use, whether their loved one gets formal treatment or not.

Why does CRAFT work? Here are some of the reasons:

- It is based on the idea that people do not use substances in a vacuum. Relationships impact substance use just as substance use impacts relationships.

- It assumes that most family members and friends have good intentions, good instincts, and a healthy (versus codependent) desire to help.

- It treats the problems that families face regarding when and how to help their substance-dependent loved one as a deficit of skills—skills that can be learned—rather than as a disease of codependence.

- It uses collaboration and kindness rather than confrontation and conflict.

The following strategies are based on CRAFT's approach, modified to make them more collaborative. However, whereas CRAFT's program encourages family members to complete these strategies on their own, even without their loved one's agreement or participation, we feel strongly that when dealing with a partner, the person should be part of the process from the beginning. Rather than try to dictate a one-size-fits-all plan, we suggest you create your own program using the aspects of each strategy that fit your needs, personality, and lifestyle. If a strategy doesn't feel like something both you and your partner will be comfortable doing, by all means, do not do it!

Strategy #1: Perform a Behavioral Analysis

As we discussed in chapter 4, a primary way to gain compassion for someone is to understand them better—including why they do what they do. A *behavior analysis* involves systematically thinking through the specifics of how and why your partner uses a substance or engages in a compulsive behavior.

This strategy is designed to help you understand your partner on a much deeper level. If done with your partner—which we recommend—it will also help your partner gain a deeper understanding of (and compassion for) himself. Understanding the reasons why your partner engages in dependent or compulsive behavior—his motivation—is also the key to helping him stop, because the problem contains the seeds of its solution. Often when a person discovers another, healthier way to feel better or to cope with not feeling good, he no longer chooses the unhealthy alternative.

Note that when we refer to your partner's motivation, we aren't just talking about deep-rooted issues such as child abuse or abandonment. We're also referring to day-to-day reasons for using substances or engaging in related behaviors. For example, your partner may drink in order to feel less depressed and anxious; he may take drugs to block out painful memories; he may gamble in order to feel an adrenaline rush that pushes away sadness. Earlier we discussed human beings' deep need to bond and form connections with others in order to feel fulfilled. Sometimes when we can't connect with each other, we connect with anything we can find—even when that connection is not real, as in the case of a man who is unable to maintain an intimate relationship with a woman and attempts to gain the same feeling of connection by calling a phone sex line. The desire for connection could be your partner's motivation to use.

A behavior analysis accomplishes six goals:

1. It gives you an estimate of your partner's current use (which can, in turn, be used to measure future changes).

2. It helps you recognize the predictability in your partner's substance use. It may feel as if his substance use is random, but there is likely a real pattern to it. Recognizing this pattern can help you stop living in fear of another episode.

3. It clarifies your partner's "triggers" (the reasons for his behavior)—including who or what triggers him and where or why he might be triggered.

4. It identifies the negative consequences of his behavior, along with the positive ones, so you can pinpoint options for changing the balance.

5. It helps you feel empathy toward your partner, as you begin to understand his use from his perspective.

6. It can be the beginning of a collaborative relationship with your partner. In fact, since you may need to ask him questions in order to complete the analysis, it can be the first step toward working together.[29]

{EXERCISE}

BEHAVIOR ANALYSIS OF YOUR PARTNER'S SUBSTANCE USE OR COMPULSIVE BEHAVIOR

Find a time and place for you and your partner to have an undisturbed discussion. The optimal way to do this analysis is for you to verbally ask your partner these questions and then write down his answers, thereby involving both of you in the process while making it clear that your role is to facilitate and observe his process. Give your partner time to think about each response and offer to help him only if he is absolutely stuck and asks for your help. The questions are divided into sections, and you may find that you get through only one section before needing to take a break or even stop for the day.

If your partner is uncomfortable doing this exercise with you, it is fine for him to do it alone and then, if he chooses, share the information with you either verbally or in writing.

Even if your partner refuses to complete this exercise, or does not want to involve you as a collaborator in his recovery, you may want to try to answer these questions yourself. This option isn't ideal, but it will still yield important information that can help you with the other strategies we offer in this chapter.

Behavior

- What substance or activity do you usually use?
- How often do you use the substance or get involved with the behavior? (every day, every week, every month, constantly)
- Over what period of time do you usually use? (a day, a week, a month, constantly)

External Triggers

- What is typically going on in the environment just before you use?
- When do you usually use?
- Are you alone or with others when you use? If you are with others, who are they?
- Where do you usually use?

Internal Triggers

- What are you generally thinking about just before using?
- What are you feeling just before using?

Short-Term Positive Consequences

- What pleasant thoughts do you have while using?
- What pleasant feelings do you have while using?
- What do you like about the people with whom you use?
- What do you like about the places where you use?
- What do you like about the time of day/night when you use?

Long-Term Negative Consequences

What do you think are the long-term consequences of using . . .

- . . . to your relationships?
- . . . to your physical health?
- . . . to your emotional health?
- . . . to your job/career and your financial well-being?

Strategy #2: Reinforce Positive Changes

Earlier we discussed the various reasons why your loved one may have become dependent on certain substances and/or activities, stressing that substance dependency is usually caused by a combination of factors, including genetics, environment, and physiological and psychological variables.

But at the core of all these factors is a *choice*, made consciously or unconsciously, each and every time the person uses. The decision to use mood-altering substances is a choice even when the behavior becomes so automatic that it no longer looks or feels like a choice. These choices are based on the results a person expects from making that choice—what he expects to feel or get. Those results can include pleasant physical sensations and emotions, or the lessening of negative emotions or anxiety—for example, feeling more relaxed after a drink or temporarily escaping from emotional pain through sex.

The chain of events whenever your partner uses goes like this: He takes an action. What follows either increases or decreases the likelihood that he will repeat that action in the future. Anything that reinforces the likelihood one way or the other is what behaviorists call a *reinforcer*.

According to the authors of *Beyond Addiction,* "Mood-altering substances (and some behaviors) are powerful reinforcers due to their effect on the brain."[30] When your partner chooses to use a mood-altering substance, he feels good; that leads him to want to choose it again.

Reinforcers can also take the form of something negative *not* happening. For example, perhaps your partner says that when he drinks, he doesn't think about the past. In this case drinking is reinforced by the absence of painful memories and the feelings that accompany them.

The good news is that reinforcement works the same way for behaviors that you *do* want to happen again. For example, let's say your husband has told you that one of the reasons he stops off at the bar on the way home from work is that he needs some downtime before facing the stress of being around the kids. Arranging for him to have a half hour of quiet time in his home office or den when he first comes home may serve the same function—and, if so, will reinforce the likelihood of him coming home for that downtime instead of going to the bar the next time. In both cases, the reinforcer is the removal of stress. You're just changing which behavior it's reinforcing.

This reinforcement of constructive, non-substance-related behavior is CRAFT's core strategy. According to CRAFT's creators, *reinforcement is the single most effective tool you have in your attempts to help your partner.*

This is where your choices come in. You can choose to respond to your partner's positive, non-using behaviors in a way that will increase the likelihood of these behaviors reoccurring. At the same time, you can choose to respond to his negative behaviors in a way that decreases the likelihood that they will reoccur.

In short, here are the two most powerful things you can do to help promote change:

1. Reward your partner for positive behavior (which we'll discuss in this section).

2. Ignore negative behavior, or withdraw a reward (which we'll discuss in the next section).

THE DIFFERENCE BETWEEN ENABLING AND REINFORCING

The term "enabling" refers to anything you do that *reinforces or increases the likelihood of your partner's substance-using behavior* or any other behavior you don't want to support. On the other hand, a positive reinforcement strategy *reinforces or increases the likelihood of your partner's positive behaviors.*

Identify Substitute Rewards

It is important that you learn how to identify activities that can compete with your partner's substance use. The next step will be to identify the rewards the two of you will choose to put into place for the behavior you want to encourage.

You probably know the Serenity Prayer: *God grant me the serenity to accept the things I cannot change, courage to change the things I can, and wisdom to know the difference.* Identifying rewards has the added benefit of helping you focus on things you *can* change, by giving you something definite and proactive to do.

The following are some general guidelines for selecting and applying rewards as reinforcers:

- *Choose rewards he will like.* Take some time to brainstorm (preferably together) about what he likes and write down as many ideas as you can. For example, he loves foot rubs, or he has a special meal he likes you to cook but it takes a long time to prepare it so you don't do it very often.

- *Choose rewards based on kindness rather than materialism.* A warm welcoming hug, a sincere thank-you, a smile, or an affectionate touch as you walk by are far superior reinforcers to buying him something he wants. They not only provide reinforcement closer to the time of your partner's change in behavior but are also likely to bring the two of you closer together and improve your relationship.

- *Don't choose rewards that are uncomfortable for you.* If a cuddle or a neck rub wouldn't feel good to you because you feel so angry with or distant from your partner, choose something a little less intimate. Reinforcement is not about pretending everything is fine. Think of another reward that he would like and you can do comfortably.

- *If you have to fake it, you shouldn't do it.* People often resist the rewarding strategy because they believe that they won't be expressing their "real" feelings—hostility, resentment, hurt—and that their partner will recognize they are faking it. But if you genuinely want to help your partner, you should be able to find a reward you are comfortable with. Remember, your "real" feelings are complicated. You may love him one minute and hate him the next—or even love him and hate him at the same time. Keep in mind that your objective is to reinforce the change you want to see, and try to connect with some genuine feelings of warmth, appreciation, and approval to reward positive behavior when you see it.[31]

- *If at all possible, choose rewards that expose your partner to healthy alternatives and healthy socializing.* If he's trying to stop smoking pot, get him a membership at a local gym where he can work out and reduce his stress in a healthy way; if he's trying to stop going out drinking with his buddies every Friday night, work together to discover an alternative activity—getting together with that nice couple you are always saying you want to see more of, going bowling with the whole family. Remember, you want to counter the isolation that often goes hand in hand with dependencies.

Identify Alternative Behaviors

The next step in creating a reinforcing environment involves identifying *specific behaviors (or activities) you want to reinforce.* But in order to do this, you first need to pinpoint what your partner gets out of his unhealthy dependent behavior (see the following "Short-Term Positive Consequences" exercise) and then identify replacement behaviors that provide the same benefits but also support health and well-being.

{EXERCISE}
SHORT-TERM POSITIVE CONSEQUENCES

Have your partner answer the following question and write down the answers: What reasons (if any) do you have for using this substance or activity? (Some answers might be to relax, to tune out, or to stop negative thoughts.) The answers to this question are the *reinforcers* that are already in place.

Next, brainstorm together to create a list of alternative behaviors with similar benefits. If one reason he gets high is to relax, alternative behaviors with similar benefits might include going for a walk or a swim, taking a nap, getting a massage, meditating, or doing yoga.

You probably have noticed that your partner's substance use occurs at certain times of the day and/or on certain days. The alternative behaviors that will be most effective at competing with this use pattern are ones that not only fill a similar function, but also can be done during the time he would have spent using. If drinking takes away his inhibitions with people and helps him socialize, on those nights he usually drinks, create other situations in which socializing is less difficult. Consider settings where substances are not allowed or readily available, such as museums, meditation groups, or yoga classes. And try to involve people who don't use or encourage use.

It is also important to brainstorm together ways to help your partner make or reinforce family and/or community connections and to build a social life that does not include substances or unhealthy activities. You may have to revisit the past in order to help your partner remember what activities he used to enjoy.

{EXERCISE}
EVALUATING REPLACEMENT ACTIVITIES

Once you have created a list of ideas for replacement activities together, have your partner answer the following questions for each alternative, in order to make sure the activity is a good option. We suggest he write down his answers.

- Would I enjoy this alternative (both the actual activity and the benefits it provides)?

- Is it possible I would receive benefits from it that I would otherwise get from using substances?
- Do I think that the alternative activity can replace the substance-using behavior in terms of providing me comfort, stimulation, etc.?
- Does the opportunity to engage in the new behavior occur often enough? (If not, look for behaviors that are routine or repeated on a regular basis, such as weekly classes or daily exercise so that continuation will make a difference over time.)
- Is the new behavior or activity something that both my partner and I can enjoy together? (Since the new life you are building includes both of you, look for activities that are conducive to the two of you spending more time together.)

Offer Extra Encouragement

In your role as collaborator, you can reinforce these replacement activities by providing rewards *in addition to* intrinsic benefits. Since substances are powerful and change is difficult, your partner may need extra encouragement, especially at first. You can offer this encouragement through the examples of kindness we talked about earlier (a hug, a kiss, an encouraging look) or by offering compassionate statements such as:

- "I know how difficult it has been for you to stop drinking. There must be times when you really suffer because of it. I want you to know I am really proud of you."

- "I appreciate the fact that you aren't spending as much time on the computer, how you turn it off and come to bed with me instead. I've really enjoyed talking to you and cuddling together before we go to sleep."

You can also offer encouragement by looking for activities, experiences, or hobbies that are positive and healthy to suggest to him or offer to him to compete with his substance use.

If You Find Spending Time Together Difficult

You may feel too angry or burned out to want to spend time with your partner. If this is the case, start small—choose activities that don't require you to talk or otherwise engage on too intimate a level, such as going to the movies or going for a bike ride together. You may also feel resistant to spending more time with your partner while he is still using. However, CRAFT studies have consistently shown a connection between enjoying time together and decreased destructive behavior on the part of the person who is substance dependent, as well as an increased sense of well-being for both of you.[32] Spending time together also enhances the collaborative atmosphere you're building, further supporting your partner's ability to change.

A word of caution: Try to resist talking about anything too serious during the time you spend together doing these alternative activities. The focus should be on spending time together that is free of stress and conflict and that will help improve your relationship. You likely have been holding in a lot of feelings, and understandably so, but this is not the time to discuss them. Talk to a friend or practice self-care strategies instead (see chapter 10). You will have other opportunities in the future to share your feelings or have more serious conversations with your partner.

Strategy #3: Provide Negative Consequences

Just as you paired positive consequences with positive behaviors to encourage them, you can apply (or allow) negative consequences with negative behaviors to *dis*courage them.

It takes time to stay sober instead of using, to learn to exercise instead of dealing with stress with substances, to leave work instead of continuing to work compulsively, to stop gambling and take up a healthier habit. In the meantime, the following strategies will help you discourage behaviors in your partner that you have both agreed you want him to stop. They are not mutually exclusive, and can be combined for even greater impact.

Hold Back the Reward You Have Been Using

Pick something you can withdraw during or immediately after the negative behavior occurs. This will immediately strengthen the link between the behavior and the consequence. For optimum effectiveness, you will need to reinstate the reward when the positive behavior returns. This may mean that you will need to put aside your hurt or angry feelings about the past slip.

Remember, *holding back a reward is not punishment*. Punishment is doing something *to* a person; taking a time out from positive reinforcement is simply not giving something that you gave previously for positive behavior. It's also temporary—the reward will be given again very soon. But holding back a reward allows you to respond to negative behavior in a way that avoids a fight or other negative action on your part, leaving it up to your partner to learn the consequences of his choices.

For example, your partner may have told you that one reward he would like is a home-cooked meal on Saturday nights. You may have agreed to do this as long as he continues to not smoke pot. So, on a night when you come home to the smell of pot in the house, instead of confronting him about his slip, yelling at him, or giving him the silent treatment, you simply say, "Oh, I see that you've smoked pot today, so I'm not going to cook this Saturday. You can go for take-out or we'll eat leftovers."

It is your choice whether you tell your partner about your plan to withhold a reward or not, but communicating your plan can help reduce the emotionality of your partner's response.

Allow the Natural Negative Consequences That Result from a Negative Behavior

Natural consequences are the direct outcomes of your partner's substance use that he would experience if no one interfered or rescued him. These outcomes can include emotional costs such as shame, loss of control, anger, or depression; physical costs such as loss of sleep, hangover, poor health, or injury; and other costs such as loss of relationships, loss of a job, financial difficulties, and legal problems. For example, if your partner wakes up too hung over to go to work after a night of drinking, don't call his boss for him and say that he is sick.

Note that just as a reward is only as reinforcing as its value to the person receiving it, a consequence will impact your partner only if he experiences it as a drawback. If your partner hates his job and is looking for a new one, he won't view losing it as a negative consequence. In order to be effective, negative consequences need to be compelling reasons for your partner to stop his current behavior.

As you allow your partner to experience these natural consequences, be aware of your facial expression, your tone of voice, and your body language. This strategy works best if you are as matter of fact as possible rather than becoming angry or righteous; you certainly don't want to say (or imply) *I told you so*. A punitive attitude interferes with the collaborative relationship necessary for positive change.

If done correctly, this strategy helps your partner focus his or her stress, frustration, and resistance *within himself*, rather than between the two of you. Allow him to come face to face—the literal meaning of "confront"—with the results of his own actions instead of blaming you.

Ignore the Negative Behavior

Ignoring your partner's behavior gives the least amount of reinforcement possible—no reward, no response, no attention at all. Typically, when a behavior is not reinforced, it is gradually extinguished.

Don't confuse this with giving the cold shoulder or the silent treatment, or other ways of communicating displeasure. Ignoring says *I am not interested in this behavior*, whereas giving the cold shoulder says, *I'm angry with you.*

It is not recommended that you ignore substance use very often, as withdrawing rewards and allowing consequences are more effective strategies. Ignoring is helpful for dealing with your partner's reactions to the other strategies, however—particularly if your partner begins swearing, sulking, or yelling, or says some version of "Why are you doing this to me?!" If you respond to these negative reactions in any way, you in essence reinforce them.

A word of warning: Sometimes ignoring a behavior initially results in an escalation of the behavior, a phenomena referred to as *behavioral burst.* This doesn't tend to last very long and can actually signal an upcoming end to the behavior. The best way to deal with this period is to just ride it out, because if you respond to a burst, your partner may learn that if he pushes you hard enough, you will give in—that his behavior (swearing, sulking, yelling) still works. The most effective way of dealing with a burst is to ignore it and then, the moment he stops, to give him positive reinforcement in the form of your attention.

If You Are Uncomfortable with This Strategy

You may feel uncomfortable with strategy #3—if so, you aren't alone. Many people don't like thinking of themselves as a "trainer" of someone they love. Some feel this behavioral approach is manipulative or dishonest. But having a specific plan for change that you and your partner have both agreed to isn't the same as scheming or manipulating. In fact, there is evidence that a behavioral approach is one of the most respectful, authentic ones you can use, as it takes a fundamentally collaborative, nonjudgmental approach to learning and change.[33]

Think of it this way: We influence each other in every interaction we have; reinforcement takes place between people all the time, whether it is done consciously or unconsciously. You are probably already trying to influence your partner's behavior by giving him the silent treatment or yelling at him as forms of punishment. Unfortunately, these kinds of responses create a negative reinforcement loop. As you obsess about your partner's problem and carry your distress around with you, you naturally end up nagging, withdrawing, and behaving in other punishing ways—*even when he is not using*. Your anger about the last time he used can spill over to the next day, or even days later. It is not uncommon for people with substance problems to get the same punishing reaction whether they are using or not.[34]

Not only does this kind of behavior not work to decrease the substance use, it can influence your partner's decision to continue using. He may reason that since he gets yelled at when he uses and yelled at when he doesn't, there's no reason *not* to use.

Some of the CRAFT program strategies may feel more comfortable or applicable for you and your partner than others, so start off with the most useful ones. Then let these strategies spark other creative ideas for how you and your partner can collaborate to help him recover.

CHAPTER 10

Creating Your Own
Self-Care Program

*"Self-nurturing means, above all,
making a commitment to self-compassion."*
—JENNIFER LOUDEN, *The Woman's Comfort Book*

FOLLOWING THE ADVICE AND STRATEGIES OFFERED IN THE LAST
few chapters means you will be focusing a great deal of attention on
your partner and his recovery. But as you help your partner recover,
it's important to take care of your own needs as well. Otherwise you
run the risk of "losing yourself" in your partner and his problems,
or at the very least getting burnt out and not being able to be there
for him.

Supporting or collaborating with your partner in his recovery
process isn't easy. You may feel good one day because your partner
is doing well and bad another day when he slips up. But this gives
your partner and your relationship too much power over your emotions and your life. You need to have a separate life, and that includes
focusing some of your energy on taking care of yourself.

When you take care of yourself, you build the emotional strength needed to accept what you can't change about your partner and to weather the ups and downs of his recovery process. And by caring for yourself—including taking the time and space to work on any issues of your own—you also model healthy behaviors for your partner and contribute to a healthier atmosphere in your home.

That's why we've chosen to end this book with a chapter that helps you create a personalized self-care program.

In chapter 4 we discussed the benefits of viewing your partner in a trauma-sensitive way. But partners of those who suffer from substance or activity dependence can benefit from viewing *themselves* in a trauma-sensitive way as well. As we've discussed, partners are often dependent themselves—on taking care of, rescuing, and making excuses for their partners, or on being in control of people and things outside themselves.

Understanding codependency as a behavior—or, rather, a pattern of behaviors—that helps you cope with trauma or negative feelings can grow your self-understanding and the self-compassion that comes with it. It can also help highlight the importance of taking the self-care steps necessary to feel comforted and more in control of yourself.

For some of you, creating a personalized self-care program may be a fairly easy task. You may need only the suggestions we make and the exercises we offer as reminders for you to focus more on your own needs. But for others this will be a more difficult chapter. It can be painful to realize that you don't know what you need and that even when you do, you don't know how to go about providing these things for yourself.

This is especially true if your needs were ignored or neglected when you were a child or if you were made to feel you were being "selfish" if you focused on them.

> **Chris**: *I grew up in an environment where the ethic was public service—doing for others who were less fortunate, giving*

back, and making a difference in the world by getting out of yourself and helping somebody else. There was no room for self-examination. Addressing one's own feelings was thought to be a waste of time; people were uncomfortable with it. Most folks don't like self-examination because they fear it will reveal aspects of themselves and their lives they would rather not see.

However, my instinct growing up was to examine what was happening inside myself as well as outside. The inner journey has always held more gravitas and meaning for me. I came into this world with the belief that if you change yourself for the better, you can change the world for the better. Writing my memoir was my coming out, my public emancipation from the ethic that avoidance of the inner struggle was most useful. And I was not disappointed; it led to my emancipation from much of my family legacy that didn't serve me, as well as delivering me to my work as an advocate for those struggling with addiction around the world. But it took a lot of work to get there.

If your needs or feelings were ignored or neglected, take notice of any resistance you have to our suggestions and offer yourself self-compassion instead of criticism and impatience. For example, say to yourself, "It is understandable that I would find it difficult to focus on my own needs because I was raised to focus on the needs of others."

As you read this chapter, feel free to pick and choose which suggestions feel most helpful to you in creating your own individualized plan for self-care.

RESILIENCE, NEEDS, AND SELF-AWARENESS

Resilience is the ability to maintain equanimity, health, strength, and happiness after a crisis, setback, or disappointment. It is the ability to bend without breaking, or bounce back, in the face of a challenge.

Although you cannot control your partner and, for the most part, you cannot control what challenges you will face on a daily basis, there are things you can do to help control the way you respond to both. By making sure you take care of your needs, from the most basic (food and rest) to things like companionship and stimulation, you can reduce your vulnerability to bad moods, lost tempers, and meltdowns.

The first step to being able to take care of your needs is self-awareness—that is, knowing what your needs are by being aware of your thoughts, feelings, and physical state. According to Daniel Goleman in his groundbreaking book, *Emotional Intelligence: Why It Can Matter More Than IQ*: "Self-awareness—recognizing a feeling as it happens—is the keystone of emotional intelligence [and] crucial to psychological insight and understanding . . . People with greater certainty about their feelings are better pilots of their lives, having a surer sense of how they really feel about personal decisions."

Connecting with your emotions is an essential step in connecting with your real self. Unless you know what you are feeling at any given moment, you are not in touch with who you are. It is also one of the most effective ways of moving from an external focus (people and tasks outside yourself) to an internal one. Feelings—good and bad—provide us with valuable information that can give us clues as to what our needs are, whether they are being met, and, if not, how we can meet them.

{EXERCISE}

CONNECTING FEELINGS WITH NEEDS

The following exercise will help you make the important connection between feelings and needs:

1. *Check in with yourself several times a day by asking yourself what you're feeling.* It's easier at first to stick

with the four basic feelings of anger, sadness, fear, and guilt/shame. Ask yourself, "Am I feeling angry?" If the answer is no, move on to "Am I feeling sad?" and so on. (Of course, you may find that your answer to "What am I feeling?" is something else entirely, like "lonely" or "hungry.")

2. *When you find a feeling, look for the corresponding need.* Ask yourself, "What do I need?" Answer in the simplest way rather than confusing the issue with too many details or complexities.

   Often the answer will be "I just need to feel my feeling and then let it fade." But if you feel angry, you may need to speak up for yourself. If you feel sad, you may need to cry. If you feel hungry, you need food. If you feel guilty, you may need to apologize.

   You might have to "try on" several needs before you find the one that's true for you in any given moment. You may also have many needs attached to a single feeling. For example, if you feel *lonely*, you may *need* to call a friend, to get a hug from your partner, or to connect with yourself—or all three.

3. *Be on the alert for answers that are not truly responsive to your needs.* Some examples are "I feel sad, so I need some candy" or "I feel angry, so I need to hit him." Ask yourself, "What do I *really* need?" The best answer might be "to express myself" (write, sing), "to get physical" (walk, stomp), "to develop a plan," or "to learn from the experience for next time."

Another important aspect of discovering what you need is becoming clear about what makes you feel happy, comfortable, and at peace, which the following exercises will help you focus on. Only when you know what makes you feel good can you begin to provide it for yourself!

{EXERCISE}

CONNECTING FEELINGS WITH NEEDS

1. What activities bring you the most joy?
2. What memories bring you the most joy?
3. What environment brings you the most peace or relaxation? (Examples: the beach, the garden)
4. What person or people help you feel the most accepted and loved?
5. What do you do on a regular basis that makes you feel good physically? (Examples: eating right, getting lots of sleep, exercising)
6. What do you do on a regular basis that makes you feel bad physically? (Examples: eat too many sweets, drink too much alcohol, smoke cigarettes)
7. What do you do to nurture your body? (Examples: put on lotion, do yoga, have orgasms)
8. When are you most comfortable in your body? (Examples: after exercise, lying on your bed surrounded by lots of pillows, taking a hot bath)
9. When are you most uncomfortable in your body? (Examples: when you have eaten too much, when you have to sit too close to someone else)
10. What foods make your body feel especially good?
11. What foods make your body feel uncomfortable?
12. What kind of massage do you prefer—soft and gentle, or firm and deep? What kind of touch feels most loving to you when your partner touches you—soft, slow, firm, comforting?
13. Do you prefer a bath or a shower? Do you like to sit in a really hot tub or Jacuzzi, or does this bother you?
14. What kinds of music do you prefer when you want to relax and connect with your feelings? Do you resist music that might make you feel sad because you don't want to cry? If so, is there a type of music or sound—such as soft jazz or environmental sounds—that can help you relax without causing you pain?

Based on your answers to these questions, begin to make a list of activities, places, and people that help you feel peaceful, relaxed, joyful, and loved.

{EXERCISE}
YOUR FEEL-GOOD JOURNAL

Buy a journal or create a folder on your computer and begin to jot down when you are feeling especially good—physically, emotionally, or spiritually. Pay particular attention to the circumstances surrounding these good feelings. You may notice that when you are with a certain person—a friend or loved one—you feel especially open and loving. Note this in your journal. You may notice that certain things in your environment make you feel happy—such as looking at the ocean, watching a sunset, seeing beautiful flowers, or being around animals. Write it down. You may also notice that when you act a certain way you end up feeling really good about yourself—for example, when you take the risk of being honest with someone, when you put your criticism of someone aside and feel real compassion for the person, or when you stop to give yourself credit for accomplishing something difficult. Write it down. Then periodically go back and read your Feel-Good Journal as a reminder to repeat these activities.

WHY YOU MAY HAVE TROUBLE CONNECTING WITH YOUR FEELINGS

If you experienced constant chaos in the home as you were growing up, as is often the case in alcoholic families, emotions may be frightening things for you. If you witnessed your parents' emotions getting out of hand or if you got yelled at, pushed around, or hit when a parent was angry, you may have come to fear emotions. And if you were ridiculed, punished, or abandoned when you got angry or started to cry, you may have learned to deny and repress your true emotions. Despite appearances, some people who are extremely emotional, including those who are eruptive or volatile, often respond so strongly only because they are denying more vulnerable feelings underneath. Those with a history of neglect or abuse also tend to be overwhelmed and controlled by their emotions; it can feel as if their emotions have become their enemies.

Dysfunctional behaviors, including abusive or victim-like patterns, codependency, substance abuse, and suicidal tendencies, are often attempts to cope with intolerably painful emotions. Many people with codependent behavior patterns try to regulate their emotions, attempting to make themselves not feel whatever it is that they feel. This can be a direct result of an emotionally invalidating environment—one that mandates that people should smile even when they are unhappy, be nice and not rock the boat when they are angry, and beg for forgiveness even when they don't feel they did anything wrong.

If as a child your feelings weren't honored, you may have stopped feeling them—to the point that you now have trouble feeling or identifying emotions as an adult. If your feelings weren't validated, you may have difficulty believing even today that you have the right to them. Because of this, you may often feel sideswiped by your own emotions, or overwhelmed when they build up. This in turn may cause you to project your feelings onto others—for instance, accusing your partner of being angry with you when, in actuality, you are the one who is angry with him.

Finally, you may be unaware of what you are feeling at any given time. This lack of awareness makes it difficult for you to cope with any feelings that suddenly erupt in you. Since you don't know what you need, you will be unable to communicate your needs to others. This means you will end up doing things you don't want to do, being around people you don't really care for, and, in terms of your partner, putting up with behavior you shouldn't put up with.

One possible reason for this disconnection is trauma experienced in childhood, whether abandonment, neglect, abuse (physical, emotional, or sexual), or loss of a loved one. Children (and adults) shut off their feelings, or *dissociate*, in response to traumatic situations. This dissociation can be experienced as feeling "spaced out" or dizzy, or feeling a floating sensation, as if the ground is slipping away. Some experience it as a feeling of detachment, as if their mind goes somewhere else and they are disconnected from their body. Others experience it as a feeling of mental or emotional numbness or deadness, or simply a lack of connection with themselves—which is exactly what it is.

Some people experienced so much trauma, chaos, or unpredictability in their childhood (for example, if their parents were constantly fighting, or they never knew when an alcoholic parent would suddenly have a violent outburst) that they developed a habit of dissociating. As adults they slip into a dissociative state whenever there is the slightest hint of upset. If you tend to dissociate as a result of traumatic childhood experiences, you will need to practice the following grounding exercise on a regular basis in order to break your habit of dissociating and bring yourself back to the present moment.

{EXERCISE}
GROUNDING PRACTICE

1. Find a quiet place where you will not be disturbed or distracted.
2. Sit up in a chair or on a couch. Put your feet flat on the ground. (If you are wearing shoes with heels, take them off.)
3. With your eyes open, take a few deep breaths. Turn your attention to feeling the ground under your feet. Continue breathing and feeling your feet flat on the ground throughout the exercise.
4. Now, as you continue breathing, take a look around the room, scanning slowly, making sure you are actually seeing

what is around you. Notice the colors, shapes, and textures of the objects in the room. If you'd like, turn your head as you scan for a wider view.

5.   When your attention wanders, bring your focus back to feeling the ground under your feet as you continue to breathe and to notice the colors, shapes, and textures of the objects in the room.

6.   After you have grounded yourself, you can reassure yourself that you are safe by reminding yourself that the traumatic event is not occurring now. You can say to yourself, "I'm safe now. I'm in the present and everything is okay."

This grounding practice serves several purposes: It brings your awareness back to your body, which can stop you from dissociating. It returns you to the present, in case a trigger has catapulted you into the past. And it deliberately focuses your attention elsewhere, which allows strong feelings and thoughts to subside to the point where they are not dominating your experience.

MEETING YOUR OWN NEEDS

If you are going through a hard time while supporting or collaborating with your partner, instead of obsessing about what your partner did or did not do, ask yourself what you need in order to cope with the situation. Write down what you can provide for yourself (as opposed to what you want or need from your partner). For example, if your partner comes home after a night out drinking and criticizes you, instead of thinking, "What I need is for him to apologize to me for the way he talked to me," try focusing on how you can make yourself feel better: "What I need is to remind myself that I am not the things he says I am. Then I need to talk to myself in a loving, kind way and remind myself of my positive qualities."

BASIC SELF-CARE STRATEGIES

The following list of basic self-care strategies may seem self-evident. Eat, drink, sleep—of course we all know we need to do these things. Yet the partners of those dependent on substances or activities often put even the most basic self-care needs on the back burner, especially when stressed or in the midst of a crisis (such as your partner getting arrested for drunk driving).

It's easy to tell yourself that you will start an exercise program or catch up on your sleep in the *future*—when you have more time, when the crisis is over. But self-care is not a luxury to be deferred until your partner is handling things better; it is something you need to do *now* to make things better for both of you.

These are the most basic—and most necessary—self-care strategies:

- Eat regular meals of nutritious food.
- Drink plenty of water—not diet cola or coffee, but water.
- Get plenty of sleep.
- Get regular exercise.
- Reach out for connection and companionship when you feel isolated and lonely.
- Provide yourself with healthy sexual outlets. This includes masturbation, especially if your partner is unable or unwilling to engage in sexual activity with you or you do not feel close enough to him to engage in sex with him.
- Provide yourself with adequate stimulation. Get involved in activities that fuel your mind, body, and spirit.
- Satisfy your need for spiritual sustenance, whether in the form of contemplation, gratitude, prayer, ritual, study, or some other expression.

- Take care of your medical needs, including visiting your doctor for well visits and treating illness (taking medications as prescribed, staying home and resting when sick).

MANAGING YOUR TRIGGERS

Another important aspect of self-care is learning what your triggers are and finding ways to manage them.

A trigger is anything that sets off a memory or flashback that transports a person to the event of the original trauma. This is a normal occurrence for those who suffer from PTSD. When a person is "triggered," he or she reacts spontaneously and intensely, often without realizing what caused the reaction.

The following is a list of the most common triggers experienced by those who suffered neglect or abuse in childhood:

- *Perceived abandonment.* If you had childhood experiences with abandonment or neglect, you may be acutely sensitive to any hint of perceived abandonment by your partner and likely react powerfully and sometimes violently. For example, even the slightest hint of disapproval from your partner can trigger powerful feelings of rejection. When you see your partner laughing and being happy with someone else, you may feel certain that he is having an affair or that he is planning to leave you for her.

- *Feeling criticized.* If you were regularly criticized or shamed by your parents or other authority figures, you may react very intensely if you feel criticized today. This may happen for several reasons. First of all, you may carry around a great deal of shame, so whenever you are criticized you become overwhelmed with shame. Another reason you may be triggered by criticism is that you may see things in all-or-nothing terms, and when you are criticized it can make you feel shame for being "all bad." Finally, criticism can feel like rejection and can therefore trigger a fear of abandonment. Your thinking may go like this: *If you don't like something I've done, it means you don't like me and you are going to abandon me.*

- *Feeling that others are unpredictable.* If you grew up in an environment where there was a great deal of chaos or inconsistency, you may have a great need for consistency and predictability, especially from those close to you. This can be true even if you are often unpredictable yourself. When you experience a person or situation as being inconsistent or unpredictable, this may cause you to be fearful and anxious. This particular trigger can also trigger a fear of abandonment, since unpredictability often goes hand in hand with rejection or abandonment.

- *Feeling invalidated or dismissed.* If your feelings were not validated when you were growing up, you may not have developed a strong sense of self, so you may be especially sensitive to comments or attitudes that are invalidating or dismissive. Comments like "You're overreacting" or "You shouldn't feel like that" serve to deny your feelings and thoughts.

- *Envy.* If your parents seemed to favor a sibling over you, you may be overwhelmed with feelings of envy when someone else receives special recognition. This can cause you to feel depressed or to act out in order to draw attention to yourself. This can happen during celebrations when all the attention is focused on someone else or even during a crisis when someone else needs the support of others. For example, instead of being supportive when your partner is grieving the death of a family member, you may criticize him for being too needy or you may even create another crisis so that your partner will be forced to take care of you.

• *Feeling smothered.* If you had overly controlling or overly protective parents, or if you had an emotionally needy parent who expected you to meet his or her emotional (or sexual) needs, you may be triggered whenever someone invades your physical or emotional space, demands something you don't feel equipped or willing to supply, or pressures you for sex or affection.

Ask yourself if it is possible that you become triggered when any of these situations arise. Sometimes what upsets you most about your partner's behavior is that what he said or did reminds you of another time and place—often something from your childhood. For example, imagine that your husband doesn't come home for dinner (again). In addition to sparking feelings of disappointment, anger, or fear because of the present situation (you want your husband to eat dinner with the family since he doesn't spend enough time with the children; you are afraid he has been in an accident), it may have triggered memories of your father not coming home, your mother ranting about it for hours, and the violent arguments that ensued once he got home.

Once you realize you have been triggered by the past, the fastest and most effective way to bring yourself back into the present is to ground yourself. The grounding practice exercise on page 177 can help bring you back to the present when you have been triggered by something that reminds you of past trauma.

OBSTACLES TO SELF-CARE

Even after you get in touch with what you need, you may find you still have trouble giving it to yourself. Perhaps you feel that you don't deserve to take care of yourself, that it is selfish or even unacceptable, depending on your childhood history. If your basic needs were not met, you may have a difficult time knowing how to meet those needs now. You may have a disconnect between being aware of what you need and determining how to provide it for yourself.

A child needs to receive love in order to be able to feel love; this includes love for oneself. If we do not love ourselves, we will not be motivated to take care of ourselves. Those who were neglected or emotionally abused often look at those who are motivated to take care of themselves with wonder, poignantly aware that there is some-thing missing in them, something that would otherwise allow them to say no to a second piece of cake, or get out of bed at six o'clock in order to get to the gym before work, or leave an abusive partner. That something that is missing is self-love.

Others care for their bodies but do not care for their emotions or their souls, sometimes devoting so much time to worrying about how they look on the outside that they lose track of who they are on the inside. They can spend hours working out at the gym but not even five minutes checking in with how they feel.

Some adults who were neglected or emotionally abused do not take care of themselves because they do not feel they deserve it. Chil-dren tend to blame the neglect and abuse they experience on them-selves, in essence saying to themselves, "My mother is treating me like this because I've been bad" or "I am being neglected because I am unlovable." Adult survivors often continue this kind of rationalization, and find themselves putting up with poor treatment by friends, bosses, and romantic partners because they believe they brought it on themselves. They feel so unworthy that they actually feel uncomfortable when good things happen to them—and with the idea of providing good things for themselves.

{EXERCISE}

YOUR REASONS FOR NOT TAKING BETTER CARE OF YOURSELF

1. List all the ways that you deprive yourself of nurturing, support, protection, and pleasure.
2. Write down the reason or reasons why you believe you do not take better care of yourself.

Many survivors of neglect and emotional abuse treat themselves exactly the way their parents did. They are so used to being deprived, abandoned, controlled, shamed, or ignored that they end up depriving, abandoning, controlling, shaming, or ignoring themselves in many of the same ways. But if this describes you, you do not have to stay trapped in the patterns you learned from your parents.

Some people believe that if they indulge themselves now—by, for example, overeating or overspending—they can make up for the neglect and deprivation they experienced as a child. But although it's tempting to indulge yourself in order to make up for what you did not receive as a child, this will not change the deprivation you experienced. The only thing that will begin to make up for what you did not receive as a child is for you to become the responsive, nurturing parent to yourself that you deserved all along.

{EXERCISE}

IF YOUR PARENTS NEGLECTED YOUR NEEDS

1. Write down examples of how your parents neglected to take care of your basic needs. Focus especially on how they deprived you of comfort, protection, or nurturing.

   One client of Beverly's wrote: "My parents were always impatient with me, hurrying me around, yelling at me to hurry up. I always felt that I was in the way or that I was irritating them when I tried to tell them about my day at school."

2. Notice how often you treat yourself in similar ways to how your parents (or other caretakers) treated you.

   The same client wrote: "I realized that I am always impatient with myself. I'm always telling myself to hurry up and am always angry with myself for running late. And I always have a voice in my head that tells me to shut up whenever I feel like sharing with others."

3. Write down some ideas for how you can begin to treat yourself with more kindness in order to break these negative patterns.

   The client then wrote: "I'm going to work on being a lot more patient with myself. I don't like to be late, so I'm going to start getting ready to go places sooner so I don't have to rush and so I won't be critical of myself for running late. I'm going to risk speaking up and telling people about myself more, and work on trusting that other people want to hear about me."

Beverly: *My mother neglected me in many ways, including not caring for my physical needs by failing to provide me clean clothes, teach me proper hygiene, or take me to the dentist. Because of this, I spent my early twenties learning how to care for my physical body and having dental work done. She also deprived* *me of physical affection, and this (and my sexual abuse) set me up to become sexually promiscuous. Since this was fraught with problems for me, I learned many years later that getting massages was a better way to make up for this physical deficit, and I have made a practice of getting regular massages ever since.*

WEANING YOURSELF OF YOUR CODEPENDENT BEHAVIOR

When you begin to let go of your singular focus on your partner to also focus on yourself, it is natural to try to fill that emptiness in other ways, such as busying yourself with tasks or obsessing or fantasizing about other people. But that is just substituting one unhealthy behavior for another. The best way to wean yourself of codependent behavior and to address any feelings of emptiness that may arise is to address the problem head-on. The following exercise will help you do this.

{EXERCISE}

TAKING A DAY OFF

Try this experiment: Take a "day off" from focusing on your partner, his substance issues, his recovery, or his general needs.

1. Tell your partner (and your children, if you have them) that you are taking the day off and that they will have to fend for themselves. This means that you don't want to hear any requests or complaints from them. In fact, if at all possible, ask them to provide you with complete solitude if you stay at home. If you go to a spa or a park or other restful environment, instruct them not to contact you in any way (including text messages) unless it is an emergency.

2. Notice throughout the day how often you think about your partner (and your children). Each time, bring your

attention back to yourself—how *you* are feeling, what *your* needs are, and so on.

3. Pay attention to how you feel when you attempt to think only about yourself. Do you feel selfish? If so, try to assure yourself that you have a right to focus on your own needs and desires.

4. Notice if you begin obsessing or ruminating or if you suddenly feel overwhelmed by worry, anxiety, or negative thoughts. If so, take some deep breaths and try to bring your mind to a quiet place.

5. Notice if you begin to feel boredom, apathy, loneliness, or anxiety. If this happens, ask yourself: "What am I *really* feeling right now?" As we've discussed, it is easiest if you focus on the four primary emotions of anger, sadness, fear, and guilt/shame.

Here's what Beverly's client Rebecca reported about her "day off" to a spa:

I noticed that I felt worthless when I wasn't doing some task. I know that I keep myself busy at home so I won't feel my fear and anxiety about my husband's drinking problem. I wanted to just relax and lie by the pool, but my mind kept focusing on my husband. I wondered if he was using this time away from me to drink. I worked really hard to stop those thoughts, and for a while I was successful. But then I was overwhelmed with the feelings of emptiness and sadness.

If you feel overwhelmed with feelings of sadness or emptiness when you focus on self-care or when you try not to worry about your partner, it may be because you are disconnected from your real self—and, as we explained earlier, the best way to reconnect with yourself is by focusing on your emotions.

Without an external focus (your partner or children, your need to be productive, your worry about your partner using), you may also find that you feel worthless, depressed, and discontented, or are suddenly overwhelmed with negative thoughts. These negative thoughts are often driven by shame.

As we've shown, the best antidote to shame is self-compassion, which neutralizes shame's persistent poison. By practicing self-compassion you will find that you can begin to heal the shame you may have been carrying around since childhood.

You can also help address your feelings of depression by learning how to provide yourself with self-kindness.

PROVIDING YOURSELF WITH SELF-KINDNESS

Self-kindness means giving yourself the gifts of *patience, acceptance,* and *caring.* But it also means being tolerant of your flaws and inadequacies, instead of self-critical. And it involves learning simple tools for comforting yourself and supporting yourself whenever you suffer, fail, or feel inadequate.

Kristin Neff, the leading authority on self-compassion and the author of *Self-Compassion,* explains self-kindness as responding to ourselves just as we would to a dear friend in need—as allowing ourselves to be emotionally moved by our own pain and suffering and then asking, "How can I care for and comfort myself in this moment?"[35]

Being kind to oneself comes naturally to those who believe they deserve it. But if you've experienced a lifetime of shame, neglect, mistreatment, and/or abuse, it can make it hard for you to accept kindness from others, and even harder to believe you deserve self-kindness—much less actually begin practicing it. But if you are willing to apply the suggested strategies and complete the exercises in this section, you *will* be able to experience the healing that comes with self-kindness.

Self-kindness will be especially beneficial as you continue to act as your partner's supporter or collaborator and as you go through the ups and downs of both his and your own recovery. The kinder and more compassionate we are with ourselves, the more we can develop the courage to tolerate difficult things.

COMPASSIONATE SELF-TALK

Whenever you find yourself in a distressing situation, talk to yourself in a calm, nurturing way. You can do this silently, inside your head, or, if you are alone, you can talk out loud. Think of the kindest words you could tell yourself—the words you most need to hear.

Compassionate self-talk does not require you to come up with solutions, nor does it mean making overly optimistic promises to yourself. It is simply *an acknowledgment of your pain and suffering.* It is a statement of *comfort and validation*—an avowal that your feelings are important and that you have a right to have them.

Here are examples of compassionate self-talk used by some of Beverly's clients:

- "I know how hard this is for you. It hurts to see someone you love being so self-destructive."
- "I'm so sorry you are hurting. You don't deserve to be hurting like this."
- "I know how tired and stressed you are. You've been working so hard! It won't be long now until you are finished and you can rest."

FINDING A SELF-CARE
STRATEGY THAT WORKS FOR YOU

Whether you already practice some form of self-care or are just beginning to understand its importance, it is essential for your success at helping your partner that you discover what form or forms of self-care are best for you.

Siri Hoogen, a therapist in Portland, Oregon, and an expert contributor to GoodTherapy.org, has found that most people need "fuel" from three main sources: physical activities, cognitive activities, and emotional/relational activities.

- *Physical activities* use the body, whether you're doing something active, such as walking or running; doing something soothing, like massage or self-touch; or even doing something passive, such as sleep.

- *Cognitive activities* use the mind, such as reading, playing games, or taking a class. (Smart phones today offer a multitude of brain-challenging games and activities that may encourage your mind to stretch and exercise in ways it doesn't with everyday activities.)

- *Emotional/relational activities* include experiencing emotion (both good and bad) and engaging in social connection. Emotional refueling can mean enjoying a pleasurable emotion, such as by watching a funny TV show or reading a heartwarming book, or it may mean allowing yourself to cry. (If you know you need to cry but find it difficult to allow yourself to do so, Beverly suggests watching a movie that you know will elicit tears.) Releasing anger in a healthy way, such as "telling off" your partner when no one is around or writing an "anger letter" that you do not give to your partner, can also be useful. Relational refueling might involve sharing with a close friend or a therapist.

Although you may gravitate toward one or two of these at any given time, we all benefit from making certain that we replenish ourselves from time to time with "fuel" from each of these three main sources.

FIVE HIGHLY RECOMMENDED METHODS OF SELF-CARE

You are probably aware of many of the most popular self-care methods—for example, yoga, stretching, and deep breathing. Because these types of self-care strategies are so popular and information about them is so readily available, we won't go into them here. Instead, we are going to offer you some strategies that you might not be as familiar with.

The following methods have been found to be particularly beneficial for caregivers and partners of those who are substance dependent, based on research and feedback from Beverly's clients. Some are especially recommended for stress reduction, while others are geared more toward providing comfort and self-soothing.

Journaling

Journaling allows you to clarify your thoughts and feelings, thereby gaining valuable self-knowledge. It is also a good problem-solving tool; many of us can hash out a problem and come up with solutions more easily on paper.

Journaling can counteract many of the effects of stress. Writing about traumatic events helps us process them by fully exploring and releasing the emotions involved, which allows the experience to become more fully integrated in our mind.

Journaling as a stress-management and self-exploration tool is not the same as simply recording the events in your life in a diary. For the most helpful results, you should write in detail about your feelings and thoughts related to stressful events (such as your partner's last relapse) almost as you would discuss issues in therapy.

Music

The soothing power of music is well established. It has a unique link to our emotions and a relaxing effect on our minds and bodies. This is especially true of slow, classical music, which can have beneficial effects on physiological functions, including slowing the pulse and heart rate, lowering blood pressure, and decreasing levels of stress hormones.

Music can act as a distraction from our worries, or it can help connect us with our emotions. Listening to calming music before bedtime promotes peace and relaxation and can help induce sleep.

And it isn't just listening to music that is beneficial—singing along with music can also be a great release of tension, as can music making.[36]

Nature

Immersing ourselves in nature has both long- and short-term mental and physical benefits. Numerous studies have shown that access to trees and green spaces calms us and helps alleviate stress. By allowing our minds a respite from the typical sensory overload of a modern environment, time spent in nature tends to be restorative.

The Japanese have coined a word for a particular type of experience in nature—*Shinrin-yoku*—which means "taking in the forest atmosphere" or "forest bathing." In twenty-four field experiments across Japan, researchers found that forest environments promoted lower concentration of cortisol (the "stress hormone"), lower pulse rate, lower blood pressure, greater parasympathetic nerve activity, and lower sympathetic nerve activity in their subjects than city environments.[37]

While spending time in the forest may be particularly relaxing and healing, walking or sitting in any green space can offer many of the same advantages.

Massage

Massage is recommended for several reasons, including but not limited to the following:

- It stimulates oxytocin, which research has shown to increase feelings of calm and safety, reduce fear and anxiety, and counteract the increased blood pressure and cortisol associated with stress.
- It can help provide comfort and soothing to counteract stress.
- It is grounding—that is, massage helps you get out of your head and into your body. Those with codependent tendencies often spend most of their time in their heads—thinking, analyzing, worrying. Getting out of your head and into your body will help you get in touch with your feelings and help create more balance in your life.
- It can provide an experience of safe touch for those who were physically or sexually violated, as either a child or an adult.
- It can help provide the nurturing and sensuality you may be missing in your relationship.

Laughter and Humor

Laughter is a healthy outlet for built-up emotions and a powerful antidote to stress, pain, and conflict. Humor relaxes us, inspires hope, connects us to others, and can keep us grounded, focused, and alert. It provides us with perspective, allowing us to see a situation in a less threatening light. And it also creates psychological distance, which can help us avoid feeling overwhelmed. As Viktor Frankl, the psychiatrist, author, and concentration camp survivor, stated in his book *Man's Search for Meaning*: "I would never have made it if I could not have laughed. Laughing lifted me momentarily out of this horrible situation, just enough to make it livable . . . survivable."

You are in a situation in which you have little or no control, as it's ultimately up to your partner whether he stops depending upon his substance or activity of choice. There will probably be many dark days that give you little hope for change. Humor and laughter can lighten your burden, at least for a time, so give yourself the gift of watching a funny movie or visiting a comedy club.

There are physical, cognitive, emotional, and social benefits to humor and laughter:

- Increased endorphins and dopamine production, increased relaxation response, and reduced pain and stress (physical)

- Increased ability to cope with stress, improved problem-solving ability, and increased creativity (cognitive)

- Elevated mood and feelings of well-being; reduced depression, anxiety, and tension; increased self-esteem and resilience; increased hope, optimism, energy, and vigor (emotional)

- Bonding with family and friends, increased friendliness and altruism, happier marriages and other close relationships (social)[38]

Choose the self-care technique that attracts you the most and start practicing it. If you find that particular technique easy and fun, keep using it! If, on the other hand, you find it difficult or stressful, or just not useful, go on to try another one. There is no need to stress yourself out about it—that defeats the purpose.

If you find a particular strategy helpful, you may want to suggest it to your partner as well. It may end up helping him in his recovery. And some couples have found that practicing a self-care technique together actually improves their relationship, since it adds to the things they have in common.

Finding a way to share laughter with your partner, for example, can be extremely beneficial to the relationship. Humor and playful communication strengthen relationships by triggering positive feelings and fostering emotional connection, such as when we share an "inside joke." When we laugh with one another, a positive bond is created, which can act as a buffer against stress, disagreements, and disappointments. Shared laughter is also one of the most effective tools for keeping relationships fresh and exciting. And humor is a powerful and effective way to heal resentments, disagreements, and hurts.

Conclusion

"Love is a process, not a destination . . . a holy interpersonal environment for the evolution of two souls."
—DAPHNE ROSE KINGMAN

"A happy marriage is the union of two good forgivers."
—ROBERT QUILLEN

EVEN THOUGH THIS IS OUR CONCLUDING CHAPTER, WE DON'T want to give the impression that when you reach the end of this book, having followed our recommendations and, hopefully, helped your partner make meaningful progress in his recovery, you have reached the end of your participation in that recovery—or in your own recovery, for that matter.

If your goal has been to get your partner into some kind of a recovery program or for your partner to give up his substance or activity dependency and this has happened, you may feel that your job is over. You may feel that all you need to do now is join your partner in celebrating his success. We wish we could tell you that is the case. But this is not the end; rather, it's the beginning—the beginning of deeper individual work for both you and your partner (in the form of trauma recovery or family of origin work) or the beginning of deeper work on your relationship.

We have never known any group of people as joyous, loving, and compassionate as those who have fully engaged with therapy and/or a twelve-step program. The success that you and your partner have experienced together could be just the beginning of the incredible growth and insights you can look forward to as you continue your healing journey, both as individuals and as a couple. The potential for personal happiness, peace, freedom, and reward is limitless—as are the possibilities for your relationship to grow, get better, and become more honest and fulfilling.

But we also don't want to give you the false hope that once your partner has begun the process of recovery, your relationship issues will disappear, or your partner will magically become a more considerate, kinder, less selfish human being. During recovery, many people uncover problems that they have never dealt with or even identified before, real problems that have been hidden or masked by their substance or activity of choice.

> *Chris: Most people think that the real problem people who struggle with addiction have is dependence on their substance of choice. Others say that the addiction is a symptom of the real problem. But I say that the addiction is the solution—the addiction, no matter what it was, was the person's solution to their real, deeper problem.*
>
> *What usually happens is that when someone gets sober and comes home from a twelve-step program, his partner thinks, "He stopped using, so our problems are solved. Everything is going to be okay." But, things often get worse before they get better—if they get better at all. It's as if the addicted person has been driving around in a beat-up station wagon for twenty years, throwing all his problems and issues into the back whenever they came up. When he hits the wall and finally gets to recovery, all those problems and issues end up in his lap and he has no idea what to do with them.*

The drugs or alcohol was a way for your partner to be more amenable to and tolerant of the hardships associated with being a human being. Now that the Band-Aid has been pulled off, the recovering addict is no longer desensitized, and it takes time to develop the skills and coping mechanisms needed to deal with being human. For a while, he may be even more difficult to be around.

I want you to be prepared: There is often no "happily ever after" for some partners and couples, immediately or ever. Things may get better in terms of the police not showing up in the middle of the night or the other really toxic aspects of this illness in its active phase, but the underlying issues—sharing intimacy, being accountable, dealing with real loss—as well as the broken shoelaces of life will not be easy for a long while.

Some of us have a harder time than others just learning how to be human or how to be a real partner. Because of the culture I was socialized in, it took me fifteen years before I really understood what honesty, authenticity, and mutual respect in a marriage looked like, and recognized that they were the building blocks I wanted for my own marriage. I left my first marriage by having an affair. I would never do that today. But it's taken me thirty years to get here. Many other guys who come out of active addiction are going to be like I was.

Certainly in the beginning there can be a period of transformation and calm. But then comes the hard work, and the challenge of relearning many behaviors. I don't know anyone in recovery who hasn't needed to have a reckoning of some kind with his personal history. Many people need to adopt an entirely new operating system.

This may sound daunting, and it should! But I have seen thousands of couples transform from the misery of addiction and codependency into an honest, authentic, committed, realized coupleship. If you are reading this book, you already have the willingness to do what is necessary to have the bond with your partner you may have always imagined. Now you have the tools to make that bond a reality. The day will come when you and your partner realize that what you thought was the problem, the addiction, was actually the opportunity to transform your partnership into a relationship that is fulfilling beyond your wildest dreams.

Still, the effect on your partner, and your relationship, will depend on your individual situation.

Beverly: I have worked with many couples where once the addicted person is in recovery and no longer actively using, his partner discovers him to be a much nicer, more considerate person. In other words, there are situations where once you take away the substance or the activity, the person changes—in some instances, they change radically. They become less angry and abusive. They are less selfish, because they are able to have empathy and compassion for others, perhaps for the first time in their life. These changes take place alongside their recovery. This is especially true when the dependent person is in therapy and is working on his trauma or family of origin issues in addition to his recovery work.

I see it on a continuum. On one end of the continuum, as Chris describes, we have the people whose behavior actually gets worse once they are no longer self-medicating with a substance or activity. Generally speaking, these are people who have not been in therapy or have not acknowledged the fact that they were traumatized in childhood or have family of origin issues. They ripped off the Band-Aid only to find that there was still an open, gaping wound underneath, a wound that has been festering for years.

In the middle of the continuum we have people who once were referred to as "dry drunks" because the inappropriate behavior and "stinking thinking" we associate with substance abuse is still present, even though they are no longer using. Even though they are clean or sober, they are essentially still the same person.

And at the other end of the continuum we have those for whom the alcohol or drugs clearly affected their personality dramatically. When they give up the substance or activity, their personality changes for the better. This can be especially true of those who had anger problems or who became abusive. In some people, substances such as alcohol or drugs can cause a kind of "Dr. Jekyll and Mr. Hyde" effect, meaning that their abusive or otherwise inappropriate behavior comes out only when they are using. Take away the substance and you take away the abusive tendencies. And if the person is receiving treatment for anger and abusive behavior, there is even more of a likelihood that they will not fall back into negative behaviors—unless they relapse and once again begin using drugs or alcohol. (See my book The Jekyll and Hyde Syndrome *for more information on this syndrome.)*

Here we find those who have been working on their childhood trauma or family of origin issues for a long time, even before they entered a recovery program. Once these people become clean or sober, they usually have far less to work on in order to create and maintain a healthy, intimate relationship.

However, the following three things remain undeniably true:

1. Being in recovery from a substance or activity dependence does not resolve the emotional problems that lie underneath.

2. People respond to treatment in different ways.

3. Once a person is in recovery, the emotional problems
    that led to his addiction to begin with can exert
    themselves in new or different ways.

One final point to keep in mind: Your partner will need to continue to expend a lot of time and energy during his recovery process. And whether you have been acting as his supporter or his collaborator, a great deal of your focus has been on his recovery as well. But now it is time for you to focus on creating your own program for healing. Unless both of you continue to be active in your own recovery, your relationship cannot survive and thrive. The more you each focus on your own healing, the more you will be able to bring your best selves to the relationship—and in the process create a healthy, mutually rewarding relationship with one another.

Appendix I:
Types of Childhood Abuse

In this section we've provided a brief overview of exactly what constitutes childhood abuse and neglect in the hopes that if you were abused, this will help you get past any vestiges of denial. This section may even identify ways you were abused that you may not currently be aware of. All these forms of abuse can occur separately, but they often occur in combination; for example, emotional abuse is almost always a part of physical abuse. Also note that some behaviors fit into more than one category. For example, some neglectful behaviors can also be considered emotionally abusive.

NEGLECT

Neglect occurs when a caretaker fails to provide for the child's basic physical, emotional, social, educational, or medical needs. (Note that failure to provide for any of these needs constitutes neglect only when options are available to caretakers.)

Physical needs include providing adequate food, water, shelter, and attention to personal hygiene. Failing to provide adequate supervision (leaving a very young child alone at home while the parent is at work or otherwise away, or leaving him in the care of someone who is not fit to care for him) also constitutes neglect.

Emotional needs include nurturing, emotional security, encouragement, and validation of the child's feelings and reality.

Social needs include providing opportunities for the child to interact with other age-appropriate children.

Educational needs include providing experiences necessary for growth and development, such as sending the child to school and attending to special educational needs.

Medical needs include basic health care, including dental care and mental health treatments.

EMOTIONAL ABUSE

Emotional abuse is any nonphysical behavior or attitude that controls, intimidates, subjugates, demeans, punishes, or isolates. In the case of a child, emotional abuse consists of acts or omissions by parents or caretakers that can cause serious behavioral, cognitive, emotional, or mental disorders in the child. This includes verbal abuse (constant criticism, belittling, insulting, rejecting, teasing) as well as placing excessive, aggressive, or unreasonable demands on a child—that is, demands beyond the child's capabilities. Failure to provide the emotional and psychological nurturing and support necessary for a child's emotional and psychological growth and development (neglect) can also be considered emotional abuse.

PSYCHOLOGICAL MALTREATMENT

While psychological maltreatment is sometimes considered a subset of emotional abuse, this term is often used by professionals to describe a *concerted attack* by an adult on a child's development of self and social competence—a pattern of psychically destructive behavior that is often *more* deliberate and conscious on the parent or other caregiver's part than typical emotional abuse. Under this definition, psychological maltreatment is classified into these forms of behavior:

- *Rejecting:* behaviors that communicate or constitute abandonment of the child, such as a refusal to speak to or acknowledge the child or show affection

- *Isolating:* preventing the child from participating in normal opportunities for social interaction

- *Terrorizing:* threatening the child with severe or sinister punishment, or deliberately developing a climate of fear or threat

- *Ignoring:* being psychologically unavailable to the child and failing to respond to the child's needs or behavior

- *Corrupting:* encouraging the child to develop false social values that reinforce antisocial or deviant behavioral patterns, such as aggression, criminality, or substance abuse

- *Withholding:* deliberately withholding attention, love, support, or guidance

- *Degrading:* acts or behaviors that degrade or humiliate the child, such as making fun of their physical appearance in front of other people

- *Stimulus deprivation:* refusing to provide activities and experiences that children need for growth and education

- *Negative influence:* exposing the child to unhealthy role models (drug addicts, prostitutes, criminals)

- *Forcing children to live in dangerous or unstable environments:* for example, exposure to domestic violence or parental conflict

PHYSICAL ABUSE

Physical abuse of a child (anyone under the age of eighteen) includes any nonaccidental physical injury or pattern of injuries. This may include any of the following:

- Slapping or punching a child so hard that it causes marks or bruises.
- Kicking a child with such force that it knocks the child down or causes marks or bruises.
- Beating a child with an object.
- Burning a child with a cigarette, putting a child's hand in the fire, or other heat-related physical abuse.
- Biting a child.
- Twisting a child's arm to the point that it causes bruising or fractures.
- Shaking a child so hard it causes dizziness, disorientation, headaches, or neck, shoulder, or arm pain.
- Holding a child's head under water.
- Shoving a child against a wall, across the room, or into furniture.
- Pinning a child down on the floor and not letting them get up.
- Pinching a child so hard it causes severe pain and/or bruising.

SEXUAL ABUSE

Child sexual abuse includes any contact between an adult and a child, or between an older child and a younger child, for the purpose of sexually stimulating either partner, resulting in sexual gratification *for the older person.* This can range from nontouching offenses, such as exhibitionism or showing the child pornography, to fondling, penetration, creating child pornography, and child prostitution. A child doesn't have to be touched to be sexually molested.

The definition of "older child" is generally agreed to be two or more years older than the younger child, but even an age difference of one year can have tremendous power implications—enough to make a situation abusive. For example, an older sibling is almost always seen as an authority figure, especially if he is left "in charge" when the parents are away. His younger sister may go along with his demands out of fear or a need to please. In cases of sibling incest, the greater the age difference, the greater the betrayal of trust, and the more violent the incest tends to be.

Child sexual abuse can include any of the following:

- *Genital exposure.* The adult or older child exposes his or her genitals to the child, or forces the child to expose his or her genitals to the adult or older child.

- *Kissing.* The adult or older child kisses the child in a lingering or intimate way.

- *Fondling.* The adult or older child fondles the child's breasts, abdomen, genital area, inner thighs, or buttocks. The child may also be asked to touch the older person's body in these places.

- *Masturbation.* The adult or older child masturbates while the child observes; the adult or older child observes the child masturbating; the adult or older child and child masturbate each other (mutual masturbation).

- *Fellatio.* The child is either coerced or made to suck or place his mouth on the penis of an adult male or older male child, or the adult or older male child sucks or places his mouth on the penis of the male child.

- *Cunnilingus.* The child is either coerced or made to place his mouth in the vaginal area of an adult female or older female child, or the adult places his or her mouth in the vaginal area of the female child.

- *Digital penetration.* The adult or older child inserts a finger or fingers, or inanimate objects such as crayons or pencils, into the vagina or anus of the child.

- *Penile penetration.* The adult or older child penetrates the child's vagina or anus with his penis. In the case of a female perpetrator, the female forces the male child to penetrate her.

- *Frottage.* The adult or older child rubs his genitals or other body parts against the child's genital-rectal area or inner thighs or buttocks.

- *Pornography.* The adult or older child shows the child pornographic materials (usually done for the purpose of priming the child for sexual contact or sexually stimulating the child).

SUBTLE OR HIDDEN FORMS OF EMOTIONAL, PHYSICAL, AND SEXUAL ABUSE

Many of you reading this book already know that you were abused in childhood and that you suffer from shame because of it. But in addition to the abuse you have already identified, you may have also been abused in other, less obvious ways. Below is a description of some more hidden forms of abuse, which can be just as shaming as the more overt forms.

Subtle Forms of Emotional Abuse

In parent–child relationships, subtle forms of emotional abuse can take many forms, including the following:

- Intentionally ignoring, or withholding of attention or affection, including the "silent treatment"
- Disapproving, dismissive, contemptuous, or condescending looks, comments, or behavior
- Subtle threats of abandonment (either physical or emotional)
- Subtle forms of invalidation (not acknowledging the child's feelings or experience)
- Making the child feel in the way or unwanted
- Blaming the child for the parent's problems or circumstances
- Projecting the parent's own problems or issues onto the child
- Encouraging the child to be overly dependent on the parent
- Causing the child to feel inadequate or incapable of taking care of him- or herself

Sometimes parents deliberately shame their children without realizing the disruptive impact shame can have on the child's sense of self. Statements such as "You should be ashamed of yourself" or "Shame on you" are obvious examples. Yet because these kinds of statements are overtly shaming, they are actually easier for the child to defend against than more subtle forms of shaming, such as contempt, humiliation, and public shaming. Other examples include when behavior that has been acceptable at home is suddenly treated as unacceptable in public, or when the parent seems to be ashamed because the child is not adhering to social norms that the child was completely unaware of. Such comments as "Stop that, you're embarrassing me in front of everyone" not only cause a child to feel exposed, judged, and ashamed, but burden the child with the parent's shame as well.

There are many ways that parents shame their children:

- *Belittling.* Comments such as "You're too old to want to be held" or "You're just a crybaby" are horribly humiliating to a child. When a parent makes a negative comparison between his child and another ("Why can't you act like Tommy? Tommy isn't a crybaby"), it is not only humiliating, but it also teaches the child to compare himself to peers and find himself deficient in the comparison.

- *Blaming.* When a child makes a mistake, such as accidentally hitting a ball through a neighbor's window, he needs to take responsibility. But many parents go far beyond teaching the child a lesson, instead blaming and berating him or her: "You stupid idiot! You should have known better than to play so close to the house! Now I'm going to have to pay for that window." Blaming the child like this is like rubbing his nose in the mess he made; it produces such intolerable shame that instead of taking responsibility, he may be forced to deny responsibility or find ways of excusing the behavior.

- *Contempt.* An expression of contempt (often a sneer or curled lip), especially from someone who is significant to a child, can be a devastating inducer of shame, because the child is made to feel disgusting or offensive.

- *Humiliation.* Berating or hitting a child—especially in front of others—can serve to deeply shame the child and make him feel very bad about himself.

- *Disabling expectations.* Disabling expectations are those that pressure a child to excel at a task, skill, or activity. Parents who have an inordinate need for their child to excel at a particular activity or skill are likely to behave in ways that pressure the child to do more and more. When a child becomes aware of the real possibility of failing to meet parental expectations, he often experiences a binding self-consciousness that serves to interfere with his performance. Such messages as "I can't believe you could do such a thing" or "I am deeply disappointed in you" accompanied by a disapproving tone of voice and facial expression can crush a child's spirit. These messages are a form of disabling expectations.

Subtle Forms of Physical Abuse

Although emotional abuse usually includes only nonphysical forms of abuse, it can also include what is called *symbolic violence,* which is considered a subtle form of physical abuse as well. Symbolic violence includes intimidating behavior such as slamming doors; kicking a wall; throwing dishes, furniture, or other objects; driving recklessly while the victim is in the car; and destroying or threatening to destroy objects the victim values. Even milder behaviors, such as shaking a fist or finger, making threatening gestures or faces, or using threatening language carry symbolic threats of violence.

Such subtle physical abuse by a parent can also include keeping a strap, belt, or paddle on display for the child to see and pointing at the strap whenever the child doesn't instantly do as the parent says, or standing over the child in an intimidating way to get him to do something.

Subtle Forms of Sexual Abuse

Subtle forms of sexual abuse can include any of the following. (Keep in mind that it is the *intention* of the adult or older child while engaging in these activities that determines whether the act is sexually abusive; even if the older person never engages in touching or takes any overt sexual action, the sexual feelings that are projected are picked up by the child.)

- *Nudity.* The adult or older child parades around the house in front of the child without clothes on.

- *Disrobing.* The adult or older child disrobes in front of the child, generally when the child and the adult or older child are alone.

- *Observation of the child.* The adult or older child surreptitiously or overtly watches the child undress, bathe, excrete, or urinate.

- *Inappropriate comments.* The adult or older child makes inappropriate comments about the child's body. This can include making comments about the child's developing body (comments about the size of a boy's penis or of a girl's breasts) or asking a teenager to share intimate details about his or her dating life.

- *Sexualized touching.* Even back rubs or tickling can have a sexual aspect to them if the older person has a sexual agenda.

- *Emotional incest.* A parent romanticizes the relationship between herself and her child, treats the child as if he were her intimate partner, or is seductive with the child. This can also include a parent confiding in a child about adult sexual relationships and sharing intimate sexual details with the child or adolescent.

- *Approach behavior.* An adult or older child makes an indirect or direct sexual suggestion to the child. This can include sexual looks, innuendos, or suggestive gestures.

Appendix II:
Options for Recovery

As the partner of someone who is substance or activity dependent, your ultimate goal has likely been to encourage your partner to get into some kind of recovery or treatment program. But as we have discussed, there is no "one size fits all" when it comes to how a person recovers from a dependency.

While twelve-step programs and inpatient treatment programs are still the gold standard for many experts, others, such as the founders of the CRAFT program, believe that different people need different options and in various combinations when it comes to recovery. These options include the following:

- Inpatient treatment
- Outpatient treatment (once a week, twice a week, every day)
- Extended care facilities
- Group therapy
- Individual cognitive-behavioral therapy
- Self-help support groups
- "90 in 90" (attending ninety twelve-step meetings in ninety days)
- Sober companions

- Talking with a trusted member of the clergy
- Anticraving medication
- Medication for symptoms of withdrawal
- Treatment for co-occurring disorders such as depression or attention deficit disorder
- Self-care regimens (running or other exercise program, yoga, meditation)

There are many therapeutic options, some more supported by evidence of their effectiveness than others. But it's clear that having a choice of treatment plans leads to more positive outcomes. Giving people options helps them become invested in whatever plan they choose.

Interventions or threats such as "rehab or else" may get your partner into rehab, but coercion may kill his motivation to participate in treatment once he gets there, as well as undermine his motivation to continue making changes afterward. On the other hand, an ultimatum may not get him into rehab at all and instead may only succeed in increasing his defensiveness.

Rehab may be the best option for your partner—but it also may not be. The important thing is to help your partner find the best kinds of treatment for his or her particular problems.

Endnotes

1. Jay, Jeff and Debra Jay. *Love First: A Family's Guide to Intervention*. Minnesota: Hazelden, 2008.

2. Foote, Jeffrey, Carrie Wilkens, and Nicole Kosanke. *Beyond Addiction*. New York: Scribner, 2014.

3. Gilbert, Paul. "Introducing Compassion-Focused Therapy." *Advances in Psychiatric Treatment 15* (2009).

4. Lawford, Christopher. *Recover to Live*. Dallas: BenBella Books, 2012.

5. Foote, Wilkens, and Kosanke, *Beyond Addiction*.

6. Ibid.

7. Ibid.

8. Ibid.

9. Lawford, Christopher. *What Addicts Know*.

10. Ibid.

11. Dawson, D.A., B.F. Grant, and W.J. Ruan. "The Association between Stress and Drinking: Modifying Effects of Gender and Vulnerability. *Alcohol and Alcoholism 40* (2005).

12. Lawford. *Recover to Live*.

13. Foote, Wilkens, and Kosanke, *Beyond Addiction*.

14. Ibid.

15. Ibid.

16. Ibid.

17. Ibid.

18. Ibid.

19. Hari, Johann. *Chasing the Scream: The First and Last Days of the War on Drugs*. New York: Bloomsbury, 2015.

20. Lawford, *Recover to Live*.

21. Foote, Wilkens, and Kosanke, *Beyond Addiction.*

22. Lancer, Darlene. *Conquering Shame and Codependency.* Minnesota: Hazelden, 2014.

23. Lawford, *Recover to Live.*

24. Wray, Herbert. "The Shame of the Alcoholic." *The Huffington Post Science.* 21 Nov. 2012.

25. Neff, Kristen. *Self-Compassion.* New York: William Morrow, 2011.

26. Ibid.

27. Foote, Wilkens, and Kosanke, *Beyond Addiction.*

28. Ibid.

29. Ibid.

30. Ibid.

31. Ibid.

32. Ibid.

33. Ibid.

34. Ibid.

35. Neff, *Self-Compassion.*

36. Collingwood, Jane. "The Power of Music to Reduce Stress." *PsychCentral.* 19 Jan. 2015. http://psychcentral.com/lib/the-power-of-music-to-reduce-stress/.

37. Park B.J, Y. Tsunetsugu, T. Kasetani, T. Kagawa, and Y. Miyazaki. "The Physiological Effects of Shinrin-yoku (Taking in the Forest Atmosphere or Forest Bathing): Evidence from Field Experiments in 24 Forests across Japan." *Environmental Health and Preventative Medicine* 15 (2010).

38. "Benefits of Humor." *This Emotional Life.* 27 Jan. 2015. https://web.archive.org/web/20151017092647/http://www.pbs.org/thisemotionallife/topic/humor/benefits-humor.

About the Authors

CHRISTOPHER KENNEDY LAWFORD spent twenty years in the film and television industries as an actor, lawyer, executive, and producer. He is the author of two *New York Times* bestselling books, *Symptoms of Withdrawal* (2005) and *Moments of Clarity* (2009).

In recovery for more than twenty-five years from drug addiction, Lawford campaigns tirelessly on behalf of the recovery community in both the public and private sectors. He presently works with the United Nations, the Canadian Center on Substance Abuse, the White House Office on Drug Control Policy, and the World Health Organization. He also consults with Fortune 500 companies and numerous nonprofit groups, speaking around the world on issues related to addiction, mental health, and hepatitis C.

In 2009, California Governor Arnold Schwarzenegger appointed Lawford to the California Public Health Advisory Committee. In 2011, Lawford was named Goodwill Ambassador for the United Nations Office on Drugs and Crime to promote activities supporting drug treatment, care, and recovery. He also serves as national advocacy consultant for Caron Treatment Centers.

Lawford holds a bachelor of arts from Tufts University, a juris doctor from Boston College Law School, and a master's certification in clinical psychology from Harvard Medical School, where he held an academic appointment as a lecturer in psychiatry.

BEVERLY ENGEL is an internationally recognized psychotherapist and an acclaimed advocate for victims of sexual, physical, and emotional abuse. She is the author of twenty-one self-help books, including four bestselling books on emotional abuse: *The Emotionally Abusive Relationship*, *The Emotionally Abused Woman*, *Encouragements for the Emotionally Abused Woman*, and *Healing Your Emotional Self*. Her latest book, entitled *It Wasn't Your Fault: Freeing Yourself from the Shame of Childhood Abuse with the Power of Self-Compassion*, came out in January 2015. Beverly is a licensed marriage and family therapist, and has been practicing psychotherapy for thirty-five years.

Beverly's books have often been honored for various awards, including being a finalist in the Books for a Better Life award. Many of her books have been chosen for various book clubs, including the One Spirit book club and the *Psychology Today* book club. Her books have been translated into many languages, including Japanese, Spanish, Chinese, Korean, Greek, Turkish, and Lithuanian.

In addition to her professional work, Beverly frequently lends her expertise to national television talk shows. She has appeared on *Oprah*, CNN, *Starting Over*, and many other television programs. She regularly contributes to *Psychology Today*, has a blog on the *Psychology Today* website, and has been featured in a number of newspapers and magazines, including *O, The Oprah Magazine*; *Cosmopolitan*; *Ladies' Home Journal*; *Redbook*; *Marie Claire*; the *Chicago Tribune*; the *Washington Post*; the *Los Angeles Times*; the *Cleveland Plain Dealer*; and the *Denver Post*.

Beverly regularly conducts training workshops throughout the United States and United Kingdom for both professional and lay audiences. Recently she has been conducting trainings on emotional abuse for the United States Army, in both Texas and Georgia, as part of their domestic violence training for staff.

More from Christopher Kennedy Lawford

WHAT ADDICTS KNOW
10 LESSONS FROM RECOVERY TO BENEFIT EVERYONE

New York Times bestselling author Christopher Kennedy Lawford revisits addiction in his latest book,
What Addicts Know, this time framing the discussion in an entirely new way—the lessons addiction
and recovery offer to those of us who haven't battled
addiction.

For too long, society has considered addicts as an
unfortunate group that faces incredible and unique
challenges. The reality is that the challenges of the
addict are faced—to a greater or lesser extent—by all
of us.

In a "more is better" society, it's indisputable that
we've all experienced cravings and denied the truth
about our destructive behaviors—traits shared by addicts who've successfully
overcome them. *What Addicts Know* offers the coping and wellness skills necessary to overcome life's obstacles and self-improvement tips for everything from
conquering an unhealthy consumption of junk food, to overcoming toxic relationships. These techniques are not just for addicts; they are for all of us.

No one until now has related the lessons and life skills that can be drawn
from the collective experience of people in recovery from addiction, particularly the ways those lessons or principles can be used by those in the broader
non-recovery community. In *What Addicts Know*, Lawford recounts the inspiring
stories and wisdom of recovering addicts, combining them with cutting-edge scientific findings to give hands-on, practical techniques for recognizing unhealthy
impulses and managing them.

If you're ready to change for the better your habits, your frame of mind, your
relationships, your community, and your life, *What Addicts Know* is the resource
that will educate and inspire you along the way.

Connect with Christopher Kennedy Lawford online:
CHRISTOPHERKENNEDYLAWFORD.COM
Available wherever books are sold.